Word 98 for Macintosh

Copyright - Editions ENI - April 1999
ISBN: 2-7460-0140-3
Original edition: ISBN: 2-84072-915-6

Editions ENI

BP 32125
44021 NANTES Cedex 1

Tél : 02.40.92.45.45
Fax : 02.40.92.45.46

e-mail : editions@ediENI.com
http://www.editions-eni.com

ENI Publishing LTD

500 Chiswick High Road
London W4 5RG

Tel: 0181 956 23 20
Fax: 0181 956 23 21

e-mail: publishing@ediENI.com
http://www.editions-eni.com

On Your Side Collection managed by Corinne HERVO
This edition by Sophie CASTRO

This book is intended for users of the Microsoft's word processor Word 98 for Macintosh.

It is designed so that you can find quickly the options you need to activate and the actions you need to perform to reach the end result you require.

The screens illustrated throughout these pages add to the clarity of the explanations provided, by showing the dialog box corresponding to a given command, or by giving a precise example.

This book is made up of 11 parts.

Word 98 for Macintosh
p. 1 to 14

Basic rules for the use of the Word program and for its configuration (use of the toolbars).

Managing documents
p. 15 to 23

Commands for the management of documents (open, close, save, search...).

Entering and modifying data
p. 24 to 45

Techniques for moving around within a document, entering and selecting text, moving and copying text.

Printing
p. 46 to 55

Description of all the possibilities for previewing a document before printing and for printing (setup, header, footer).

Presentation of data
p. 56 to 80

A set of commands for formatting characters or paragraphs, and for planning their layout on the page.

Graphic objects
p. 81 to 95

Techniques for creating and managing graphic objects such as pictures, text boxes, WordArt objects...

Styles and Shortcuts
p. 96 to 115

All the possibilities for automating the presentation of data using document templates.

Revising text
p. 116 to 134

Techniques for checking in detail the contents of a text (spelling, grammar, synonyms) and also its presentation (hyphenation).

Managing long documents
p. 135 to 151

How to facilitate the management of documents using foot notes, outlines, table of contents, master documents.

Tables and charts
p. 152 to 176

Presenting numerical data in the form of a table or a chart, and calculation techniques.

**Automating
your work**
p. 177 to 201

Commands for entering data automatically, using formulas, or the mail merge technique, and also by creating macros.

In the **Appendix** you will find a list of the available combinations of keys.

In addition, at the end of this manual you will find an **index** by subject, allowing you to look up the information you need and a section on the **menus**.

**Typographic
conventions**

In order to help you find the information you require quickly and easily, the following conventions have been adopted.

These typefaces are used for:

bold

showing which menu option or dialog box to use.

italic

giving an explanation of the command you are following, or of any changes on the screen.

Ctrl

showing which keys you should press. When two keys are displayed together, they must be pressed simultaneously.

The following symbols indicate:

♦

An action you should perform (activating an option, clicking with the mouse...).

❏

A general comment on the command being used.

A tip to know and remember!

Using the mouse.

Using the keyboard.

Using the menu.

WORD 98 FOR MACINTOSH

MANAGING DOCUMENTS

ENTERING AND MODIFYING DATA

TABLE OF CONTENTS

PRINTING

PRESENTATION OF DATA

STYLES AND SHORTCUTS

REVISING TEXT

MANAGING LONG DOCUMENTS

TABLES AND CHARTS

❏ REVISING TEXT

❏ NOTES/
BOOKMARKS

❏ OUTLINES/TABLE
OF CONTENTS

❏ TABLES

AUTOMATING YOUR WORK

Starting Microsoft Word 98

♦ Double-click the Word icon. Macintosh icons are also known as "aliases".

❏ *If the Word icon does not appear on the Desktop, double-click the **Hard disk** icon, then the **Microsoft Office 98** icon, then the **Microsoft Word** icon.*

Leaving Word

♦ **File**
  Quit

♦  or ⌘ ⌘ Q

♦ If you have left any documents unsaved, Word prompts you to save them.

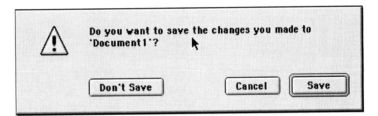

♦ Click **Save** to save, **Don't Save** to leave Word without saving the document, or **Cancel** to stay in Word.

*You can hide Word temporarily by clicking the ⓦ icon to open the Application menu and choosing the **Hide Microsoft Word** option. When Word is hidden, the Application menu icon looks like this: 🔲 Finder. To return to Word, open the menu and click **Microsoft Word**.*

**Presenting
the workscreen**

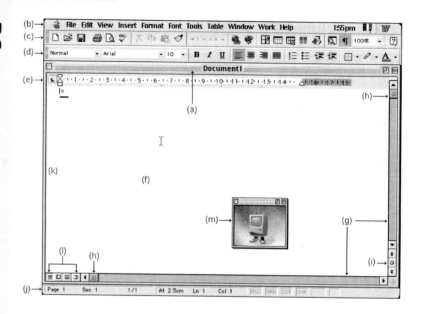

Title bar (a)

♦ The document title bar contains the **Close** box (▭), the name of the active document, the **Zoom** box (▭) and the **Collapse** box (▤) which reduces the window to its title bar.

Menu bar (b)

♦ On the left: the **Apple** menu icon along with the names of the menus in Word.
On the right: the current time, along with the **Keyboard** and **Application** menu icons.

The Standard toolbar (c) and the Formatting toolbar (d)

♦ These tools carry out certain common commands immediately: for example, saving a document.
If the bars are not visible on your screen, activate the **Standard** and **Formatting** options in **View - Toolbars**.

The ruler (e)

♦ The markers on the ruler can be repositioned to change the presentation of a text. To see the ruler on the screen, activate the **View - Ruler** option.

The workspace (f)

♦ This is the area where you enter and format text.

The scroll bars (g) and cursors (h)

♦ The cursors on the scroll bars (grey squares) indicate the position of the insertion point in the document. They are useful for looking at texts which are longer or wider than the screen.

The Select Browse Object button (i)

♦ Click this button to move around a document, from field to field, or from note to note or from title to title ...

The status bar (j)

♦ Information about the current command, or about the Word environment is displayed here.

The selection bar (k)

♦ This invisible column along the left edge of the window is used to select text with the mouse.

The view buttons (l)

♦ Use these buttons to change the current view of the document (**Normal**, **Online layout**, **Page Layout** or **Outline**).

The Office Assistant (m)

♦ The Office Assistant displays tips of general interest and help texts relevant to the task in progress.

Description of dialog boxes

A dialog box can contain up to five different elements:

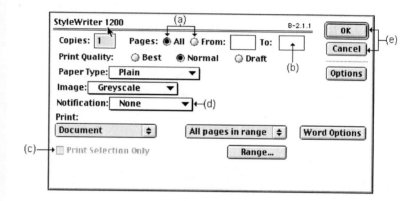

Option buttons (a): the active option has a black dot in the circle in next to it.

Edit boxes (b): when the mouse pointer is in one of these boxes, it is represented by an I with rounded corners. Once you have clicked, it becomes a flashing vertical line. Enter the data: in some edit boxes you can use **increment buttons** to choose from a list of possible values.

Check boxes (c): the choice is active when the check box has a check mark or cross in it.

Pop-up menus (d): to see the options, click the arrow button.

Command buttons (e): the **OK** button confirms the instructions in the dialog box and closes it. It is equivalent to the ⏎ key.
The **Cancel** button annuls the command and closes the dialog box; it is equivalent to the Esc key.
In many dialog boxes, related options are grouped together under separate tabs.

**Undoing
your last action(s)**

<u>One action</u>

♦ **Edit
Undo**

♦ **Z**

❏ When Word is unable to undo anything, **Can't Undo** replaces the command in the **Edit** menu.

<u>Several actions</u>

Word keeps in memory an archive of the last actions performed.

♦ Open the list by clicking the down arrow on the button.

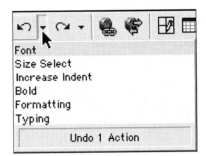

♦ Drag over the actions to undo.

❏ If the results of the cancellation turn out worse than the original mistake, use to redo what you have cancelled.

**Repeating
your last action**

♦ **Edit
Redo**

♦ **Y**

❏ When Word is unable to repeat, **Can't Redo** replaces the command in the **Edit** menu.

Using the Office Assistant

♦ If the Office Assistant is not present on the screen, click 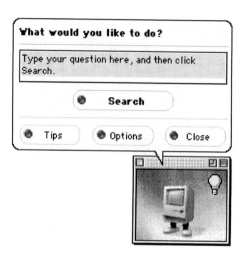.

♦ Click the Office Assistant when you need help with the job in progress.

♦ Type in a keyword and click **Search**.

♦ Select the required topic.

Word displays the help text which deals with the topic you have chosen.

♦ Once you have read the help text, you can, if you wish, display the list of the other help topics, by clicking the index button.

♦ Click ⬜ to close the window.

Changing the look of the Office Assistant

♦ Click the **Options** button in the Office Assistant window.

♦ Activate the **Gallery** tab.

♦ Use the **Next** and/or **Back** buttons to scroll through the other characters available.

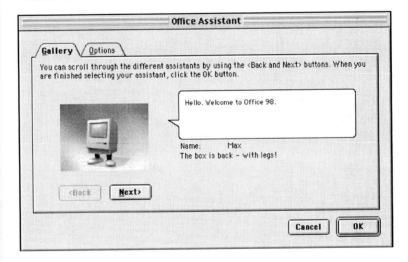

♦ When you have chosen your Assistant, click **OK**.

❏ *A light bulb in the Office Assistant indicates that Word has a tip for you. Click the Assistant to read the tip.*

Showing/hiding nonprinting characters

When these characters are visible, it is easy to see spaces, ends of paragraphs ...

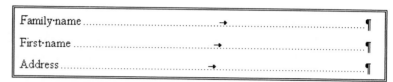

♦ Click ¶.

The nonprinting characters become visible:
¶   *represents the ↵ key,*
.   *represents the [space] bar,*
→   *represents the [→|] key,*
°   *represents a nonbreaking space.*

❏ *To hide the nonprinting characters, use the same button again.*

❏ *You can select which of the nonprinting characters to display under **Nonprinting characters** on the **View** page of the **Tools - Preferences** dialog box.*

Choosing the magnification

♦ Use the **Zoom** list box on the Standard toolbar. The list box displays the current percentage of zoom.

♦ Select one of the values proposed. The **Page Width** option displays the entire width of the page. You can also enter any percentage of your choice, between 10 and 500 %.

The new value is displayed on the toolbar.

*The **Zoom** option in the **View** menu can also be used to change the zoom.*

Changing the view

Normal view

♦ **View**
  Normal

♦  N

This view shows the text with all its formatting, but simplifies the page layout (it does not show margins, columns...).

Online Layout view

♦ **View**
  Online Layout

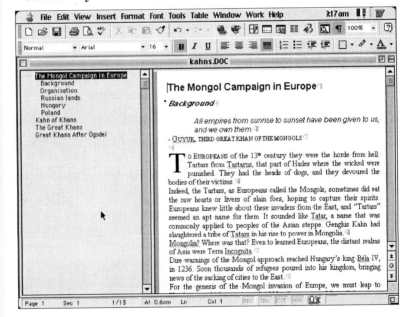

*This view is designed to make the document as easy as possible to read on the screen: the format adapts to suit the window. The view incorporates the **Document Map**, which appears as a grey band on the left of the screen.*

Page Layout view

♦ **View**   ♦ ⌘ ⌥ P
  Page Layout

This view shows the document as it will be printed.

. . . . *Personal notes* . . . .

**Displaying
an extra toolbar**

♦ **View
Toolbars**
or
Press ⌃Ctrl and click one of the toolbars.

*The standard version of Word has thirteen different toolbars, and displays two of them: **Standard** and **Formatting**.*

♦ Click the bar(s) you want to display.

❏ *Some toolbars can be displayed by clicking a button (for example,* 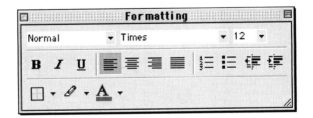 *displays the **Tables and Borders** toolbar).*

Moving a toolbar

♦ Double-click the move handle (the dotted band at the very left of the toolbar) or point to this handle and drag.

The bar becomes a "floating" toolbar: a window which can be moved and/or resized.

♦ To dock a floating bar, click its title bar and drag it to an edge of the workspace.

The window becomes either a vertical or a horizontal bar.

**Customising
a toolbar**

♦ Go into the template concerned.

♦ Display the bar you wish to customise.

♦ **View
  Toolbars
  Customize**

Removing a tool

♦ If necessary, click the **Toolbars** tab.

♦ On the toolbar itself, click the tool you want to remove, and drag it off the bar.

As soon as you release the mouse button, the tool disappears.

Restoring the original toolbar

♦ If necessary, click the **Toolbars** tab.

♦ Select the option corresponding to the toolbar concerned.

♦ Click **Reset**.

♦ Click **OK** to confirm.

Adding a tool

♦ Click the **Commands** tab.

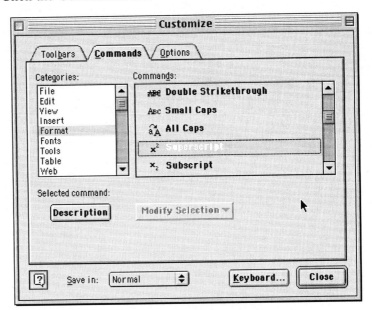

♦ Select the category of the tool in the **Categories** box.

♦ In the **Commands** box, click the tool.

*Click the **Description** button to check the use of the tool.*

♦ Drag the button you have chosen directly onto the toolbar (in the Word window).

Leaving the customising window

♦ Activate the template concerned in the **Save in** list.

♦ Click **Close**.

**Creating
a custom toolbar**

♦ View
  Toolbars
  Customize

♦ On the **Toolbars** page, click **New**.

♦ Enter a name for the toolbar you wish to create in **Toolbar name**.

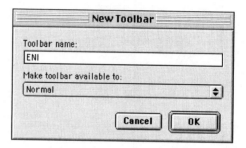

♦ Choose the template concerned in the **Make toolbar available to** list.

♦ Click **OK**.

*Your new bar is represented by a window in the **Customize** box. Its name appears at the bottom of the **Toolbars** list.*

♦ Click the **Commands** tab and add the tools of your choice, as described above in the section on customising.

♦ Click **Close**.

**Opening
a document**

♦ **File
Open**

♦ ⌥ ⌘ O

*This dialog box shows the name of the current folder together
with a list of the documents contained.*

♦ Choose the disk containing your document in the **Select a Document** pop-up menu.

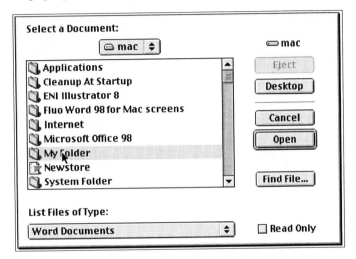

♦ To go into the folder containing your document, double-click the
folder containing your document.

♦ Double-click the document you wish to open.

**Closing
a document**

♦ **File
Close**

Click
in the document
window

♦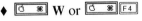

*When no document is open, only the application window appears
on the screen.*

To close all open files at once, hold the ⇧ Shift key down, open
the **File** menu, then click **Close All**.

**Creating
a new document**

To open a blank document where you can enter new text:

♦ **File**
  New
  OK

♦ N

**Saving
a document**

A new document

♦ **File**
  Save

♦ S

*The **Save As** dialog box appears.*

♦ Type the name you have chosen for the document in the **Save Current Document as** box.

The name can be up to 31 characters long, spaces included.

♦ Choose the drive where you want to store the document.

♦ Double-click the icon of the folder where you want to store the document.

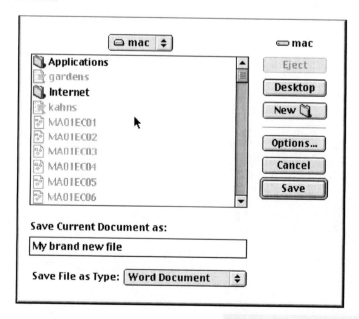

♦ Click **Save**.

❏ *The command* ***File - Save As*** *can be used to duplicate the active document under a different name.*

An existing document

♦ **File**
   Save

      ♦ **S**

While the document is being saved, a blue bar, representing the percentage saved, appears on the status bar.

❏ *To save all open documents, hold down the* Shift *key as you open the* ***File*** *menu, then click* ***Save All***.

**Protecting
a document
with a password**

Access to a document can be restricted to users who know the password.

♦ **File**
   Save or **Save As...**

♦ If necessary, enter the file name, and choose the folder where you wish to store the document.

♦ Click the **Options** button.

♦ In each **Password** box under **File sharing options for:**

  – Give a password with a maximum of 15 characters.

    You cannot see what you are typing, as the characters are replaced by large black dots (•). Be careful about what case you are using: Word differentiates between capital and small letters !

  – Enter.

    For security, the password is requested again.

  – Re-type the same password.

♦ Click the **OK** button.

♦ Click **Save**.

**Activating/
deactivating
automatic save**

If this function is active, Word saves the document automatically every so often. It is you who decides how often.

♦ **Tools
Preferences**

♦ Click the **Save** tab.

The save options are displayed.

♦ You can change the interval between each save, or deactivate the **Save AutoRecover info every** check box.

◆ Click **OK**.

Managing documents

◆ **File**
   Open

◆ O

Searching for a document

◆ **File**
   Open

◆ Click the **Find File** button.

◆ Input the various search criteria:

File Name	Specify the name of the file, if you know it.
File type	What type of file are you looking for?
Location	Specify the drive on which to search.

◆ Click **OK**.

The result of the search appears in the dialog box.

◆ Click the **Search** button if you want to change the criteria before searching again.

Using a summary to search for a document

◆ In the **Open** dialog box, click the **Find File** button followed by the **Advanced Search** button.

◆ Activate the **Summary** tab.

♦ For as many search criteria as you want:

– Input the various information requested (Title, Author, Keywords, Subject...),

– Open the **Options** pop-up menu and choose **Add Matches to List**.

♦ When you have defined your search criteria, click **OK**.

Creating a summary of the properties of a document

If you specify the title, the subject of the document, the name of the author ... it will be easier to find your document should you forget its name.

♦ **File**
Properties

♦ If necessary, activate the **Summary** tab.

♦ Fill in the various boxes.

♦ Click **OK**.

If you want Word to remind you to create a summary every time you save a new document, go into the ***Tools - Preferences*** dialog box, if necessary click the ***Save*** tab, then activate the choice ***Prompt for document properties***.

**Activating
a document
which is open
but hidden**

*Since several documents can be open at once, you often need to
activate an open document which is hidden by another.*

♦ Open the **Window** menu.

*In the lower part of this menu, the names of all open documents
are listed in alphabetical order. The name of the active document
is marked with a check mark.*

♦ Click the name of the document you wish to activate.

❑ *On the keyboard,* ⌘ ⇧Shift F6 *activates the document before
the active document, and* ⌘ F6 *the one after.*

> *To see all the open documents on the screen at the same time,
> use the command **Window - Arrange All**. To go back to viewing
> just one document, click its zoom box.*

**To insert
a document
inside another**

♦ Position the insertion point where you want to insert the document.

♦ **Insert
File...**

♦ Select the document to be inserted.

♦ In the **Range** box, specify the name of a bookmark or a range (if,
for instance, you are inserting a range of cells from a spread sheet).

♦ If you wish, activate the **Link to file** option to create a link between the active and inserted documents.

♦ Insert.

**Transferring
text from
one document
to another**

First method

♦ Select the text concerned.

♦ If you are moving a passage from one place to another:

**Edit
Cut**   ♦ X

♦ If you are duplicating:

**Edit
Copy**   ♦ C

♦ Activate the document that is going to receive the text.

♦ Position the insertion point were you want to put the text.

**Edit
Paste**   ♦ V

Second method

♦ Display both documents on the screen.

♦ To move text, drag the passage from one window to another; to copy, hold down the ⌈Ctrl⌉ key at the same time.

**Saving different
versions of the
same document**

A version is a "snapshot" of your document at a particular moment. The various versions of a document are stored in the document: no new file is created. This saves disk space.

Creating a version

♦ Go into the document concerned.

♦ **File
Versions**

♦ Click the **Save Now** button.

♦ Enter a comment which identifies the version.

❏ *If you want to create a version systematically every time you close the document, activate the **Automatically save a version on close** option.*

Opening a version

♦ **File**
  Versions

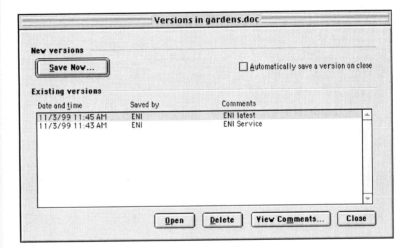

♦ Click the version you want to display.

♦ Click **Open.**

❏ *To save a version as a document in its own right, open it and use the **File - Save As** command.*

Moving
the insertion point

The insertion point is represented as a flashing vertical line. It marks your position in the document.

♦ Use the following keys to move the insertion point around:

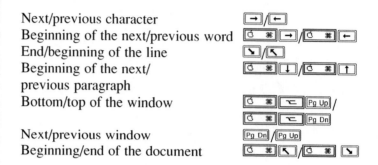

Next/previous character
Beginning of the next/previous word
End/beginning of the line
Beginning of the next/
previous paragraph
Bottom/top of the window

Next/previous window
Beginning/end of the document

These keys do not allow you to go beyond the symbol marking the end of the document.

♦ Use the scroll bars to reach the text which interests you:

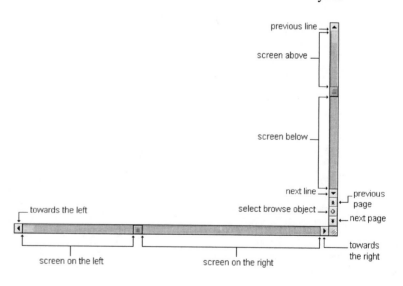

♦ To go straight to a precise point in the document, drag the scroll cursor along the scroll bar to that point's approximate position.

Word displays the page number as a ScreenTip.

♦ Click the insertion point into position.

**Moving
from object
to object
in a document**

You can jump from field to field, note to note,..., from table to table.

♦ Click the button.

♦ Click the button representing the type of object which interests you.

*The **Next** and **Previous** buttons below and above the □ button appear in blue.*

♦ Use the **Next** button and/or the **Previous** button to move from object to object.

**Using
the document
map**

♦ **View
Document Map**

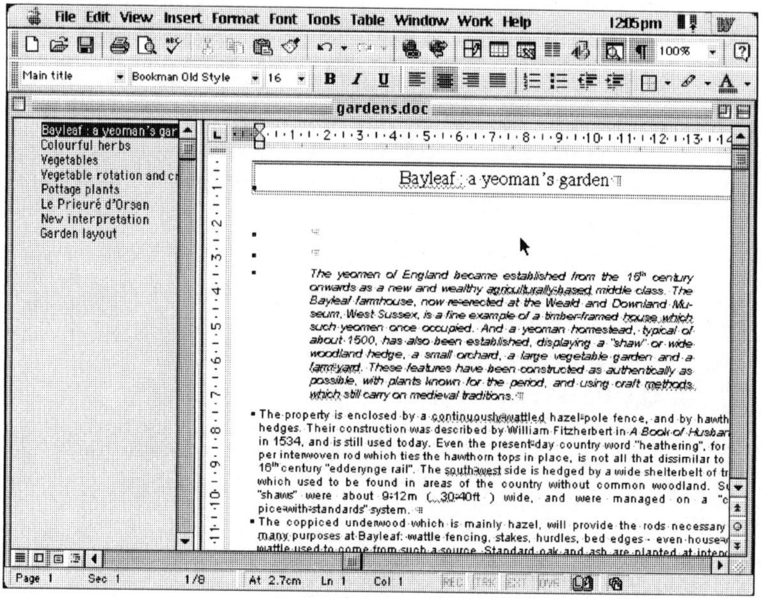

*A grey pane, called the **Document Map** or the **Document Navigator** appears at the left of the screen. It displays an outline of the document.*

♦ In the Document Map, click the part of the document you want to reach.

The part of the document that you indicate appears immediately in the pane on the right.

♦ Click 🔲 to deactivate the Document Map.

**Going to
a specific object
in a document**

♦ **Edit**	Double-click	♦ ⌃ ⌘ G
Go To	the **Page** information	
	on the status bar	

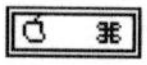

You can also click the 🔲 button then the button representing the type of item you wish to reach.

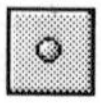

♦ Use the **Go to what** list to specify what it is you wish to reach (a **Page**, a **Section**...), then enter its number in the text box.

Alternatively, as indicated below the text box, you may move with respect to your current position by specifying the number of pages you wish to move preceded by a + to move forwards or a - to move backwards.

Enter 50%, and Word takes you to the middle of the document.

You can put several instructions together: eg. P4L10 will take you to line 10 of page 4.

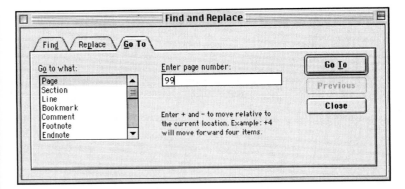

♦ Click **Go To.**

If you ask to go to a page or section, the insertion point is positioned at the first line of that page/section.

♦ Click **Close** to leave the dialog box.

Selecting text   *Different techniques are available depending on the device you use.*

♦ To select:

a word   double-click the word.

a line   point at the left end of the line (the mouse pointer takes the form of an arrow pointing top right) and click once.

a paragraph   point at the left of the paragraph (the mouse pointer takes the form of an arrow pointing top right) and double-click.

a sentence   point at the sentence, hold down the ⌘ button and click once.

the whole   point at the left edge of the text, hold down the
document   ⌘ button and click once (or triple-click the left edge of the text).

To select a group of characters:

drag   click in front of the first character to be selected, and, without releasing the mouse button, move over all the characters required. When the selection is correct, release the mouse button.

⇧ Shift -click   click in front of the first character to be selected, point after the last, hold down the ⇧ Shift key and click.

❑ *Selections are highlighted, and any new selection cancels the preceding one.*

First method

♦ Position the insertion point before the first character required.

♦ Hold down the ⌗ Shift key as you use the direction keys to select.

♦ When the selection is correct, release the ⌗ Shift key.

Second method

♦ Position the insertion point in the text you wish to select.

♦ Press F8.

EXT appears in black on the status bar: the extension of selection mode is activated.

♦ Press F8 a second time to select the word,
a third time to select the sentence,
a fourth time to select the paragraph,
a fifth time to select the section,
a sixth time to select the whole document.

♦ To return to the previous selection, press ⌗ Shift F8.

♦ Use the direction keys to make the selection more precise.

♦ Once the indicator **EXT** appears in black on the status bar, you can extend the selection by typing in the last letter you wish to select. For example, if you press ⏎, the selection is extended to the end of the paragraph.

♦ Press Esc to come out of Extension mode.

*You can also select the whole document by pressing ⌘ **A** or using the **Edit - Select All** command.*

Selecting
a column of text

This is a technique for selecting columns spaced using tabs:

♦ Drag to select (or hold down ⌞⇧ Shift⌟ as you click to select): hold down the ⌞⇥⌟ key at the same time.

or

♦ Activate the column selection mode by pressing ⌞⌘⌟⌞⇧ Shift⌟⌞F8⌟, then extend the selection as usual. Deactivate the selection mode by pressing ⌞Esc⌟.

When column selection mode is active, COL is displayed on the status bar.

. . . . *Personal notes* . . . .

Entering text
♦ Position the insertion point where you want to enter the text.

♦ Make sure the upper case lock and the number lock are as you require them.

♦ Type the text: Word takes care of the line breaks (when the insertion point reaches the end of a line, Word repositions it at the beginning of the next line).
At the end of a paragraph, press ⏎ so that the insertion point begins a new line.

When you enter the first characters of today's date, a day of the week, a month or of certain set expressions which Word recognises, a ScreenTip appears displaying the full expression. This is a case where Word's AutoComplete feature (semi-automatic data entry) comes into play.

♦ Enter if you want to accept Word's suggestion; otherwise continue typing.

❏ *To deactivate **AutoComplete**, go into **Tools - AutoCorrect - AutoText** tab and deactivate **Show AutoComplete tip for Auto-Text and dates.***

Deleting text
♦ To delete the previous character or the following character, press ← or Del. To delete all the characters between the insertion point and the preceding/next space, press ⌘←← or ⌘⌘Del.

**Correcting
an error while
you are typing**

Whenever you type a mistake, or a word that Word does not recognise, a wavy red line appears under the unrecognised word. The status bar displays a book icon marked with a cross.

♦ To correct the mistake press Ctrl and click the word concerned.

Word proposes possible replacements.

♦ Click the correct spelling.

The word is immediately replaced.

❏ Most proper nouns are not recognised by Word. Any word typed twice in a row is queried.

❏ If you do not wish red lines to appear, activate the option **Hide spelling errors in this document** in the **Tools - Preferences** menu, **Spelling & Grammar** tab. If this is done, only the icon on the status bar will indicate a mistake, and no shortcut menu of possible corrections will be available.

❏ To turn off automatic spell checking altogether, deactivate the option **Check Spelling as you type** in the **Tools - Preferences** menu, **Spelling & Grammar** tab.

Activating/ deactivating the AutoFormat function as you type

♦ **Tools**
AutoCorrect

♦ Click the **AutoFormat As You Type** tab.

♦ Under **Apply as you type**, you can choose to activate any/all of the following options:

Headings Once the option is active, if you press ⏎ once at the beginning of a paragraph and twice at the end of a paragraph, then that paragraph will be put into the style **Heading 1**. If you press ⏎ then the ⇥ key at the beginning of your paragraph and ⏎ twice at the end, it will be put into the **Heading 2** style.

Borders Once the option is active, if you type three consecutive hyphens (---) then ⏎ at the beginning of a paragraph, then that paragraph will be underlined with a single line. If you type three consecutive equal signs (===) then ⏎, the following paragraph will be underlined with a double line.

Tables Once the option is active, if you type +--+--+ at the beginning of a paragraph then ⏎, a table is created with one column for every pair of + signs (in this example: 2 columns).

Automatic Bulleted Lists Once this option is active, if you begin a paragraph with an asterisk, the > sign, a dash followed by a space or the letter O followed by a tab, then the beginning of that paragraph, and successive ones, will be marked with a bullet.

Automatic Numbered Lists Once the option is active, if you begin a paragraph with a number or letter followed by a full stop, and a space or tab, then that paragraph and successive ones will be numbered.

♦ Under **Automatically as you type**, you can choose to activate either/both of the following options:

Format beginning of list item like the one before it
If this option is active, and (for example) the first word in a list is in bold type, Word applies bold type to the first word of the next item in the list.

Define styles based on your formatting
If this option is active, Word creates new styles incorporating the formatting you have done manually.

♦ Click **OK**.

> *Deactivate the option **Straight Quotes with Smart Quotes** in the **Autoformat As You Type** frame, if you prefer to use straight quotation marks (").*

Leaving and activating insert mode

*When **Insert** mode is active, the characters you enter are inserted between existing characters.*

♦ Double-click the **OVR** indicator on the status bar.

The letters OVR on the status bar change from grey to black. They indicate that you are now in overtype mode: the characters you enter replace existing characters.

♦ To return to insert mode, double-click **OVR** again.

> *If you prefer to work in overtype mode, and just use insert occasionally, modify the standard parameters in **Tools - Preferences**: under the **Edit** tab, activate the **Overtype mode** check box.*

Changing between upper and lower case characters

You may wish to put text written in upper case (capital) letters into lower case, or vice-versa.

♦ Select the text concerned.

♦ **Format**
Change Case

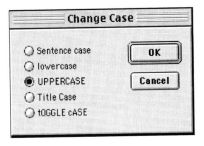

♦ Double-click the case required.

❏ *When you want to change the case of one word, you do not need to select that word: just position the insertion point in it.*

The shortcut key ⇧ Shift F3 *changes the case from upper to lower, then to title case.*

Entering formatted text

New characters automatically adopt the format which is active when they are entered.

♦ Position the insertion point where you wish to enter the text.

♦ Activate the format you require.

♦ Enter the text.

♦ Before going on, deactivate the format.

Managing paragraphs

♦ To divide a paragraph in two, position the insertion point just before the first character of what is to become the new paragraph, and press the ⏎ key.

♦ To make two paragraphs into one, position the insertion point at the end of the first paragraph and press the Del key: the character marking the end of the paragraph is deleted.

Managing blank lines

♦ To insert a line, position the insertion point at the beginning of the line which is to follow the new one, and press ⏎.

♦ To remove a blank line, position the insertion point in the line and press Del.

Using tabs

♦ Enter any text which should appear at the beginning of the line.

♦ To go on to the next tab, press the ⭾ key.

Word tabs, set every 1.25 cm, are used by default. They are marked underneath the ruler as little, grey, vertical lines.

♦ To return to the tab stop before, delete the tab character by pressing ←.

❑ *If pressing the ⭾ key or the ← key increases or decreases the paragraph's left indent, deactivate* **Tabs and backspace set left indent** *in* **Tools - Preferences, Edit** *tab.*

Inserting nonbreaking hyphens/spaces

Inserting one of these characters between two words prevents a line break between them.

♦ If the text is already entered, delete the existing space or hyphen.

♦ Insert a nonbreaking hyphen by ⌘ ⇧Shift _ or a nonbreaking space by Ctrl ⇧Shift space.

Word 98 for Macintos

❏ *When the nonprinting characters are visible, the nonbreaking space is represented by the symbol ° and the nonbreaking hypen appears as ≈.*

Inserting a date

The computer's control date should be set to today's correct date.

♦ Position the insertion point where you want the date to appear.

♦ Press [Ctrl] [⇧ Shift] **D.**

The date appears in the format DD/MM/YY.

♦ To delete the date inserted, select it and press [Del].

❏ *If* **AutoComplete (Tools - Autocorrect - Autotext)** *is active, type in the first characters of the date, and Word will fill in the rest. Press* [↵] *to insert the date.*

♦ Position the insertion point where you want the date to appear.

♦ **Insert**
Date and Time

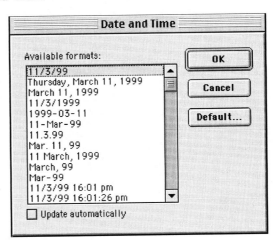

Word shows you the **Available formats** *list: it contains different presentations of the date (and time).*

◆ Click the format you prefer.

◆ If you want the date printed in your document to be updated automatically, activate the choice **Update automatically**.

◆ Click **OK**.

Inserting symbols into your text

This technique allows you to insert characters which do not figure on the keyboard.

◆ Position the insertion point where you want to put the symbol.

◆ **Insert**
Symbol
If necessary, activate the **Symbols** tab.

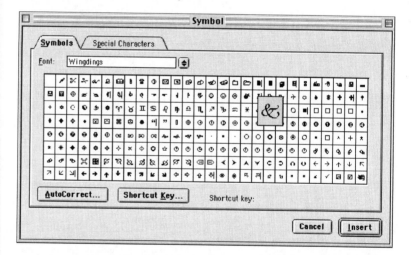

◆ In the **Font** list box, select the font containing the character you need. Depending on your printer, you may be able to use, for example, the **Zapfdingbats** or **Wingdings** font.

To zoom in on one of the symbols, click it.

◆ Double-click the character you choose to insert.

♦ Use the **Close** button or the Close box () to shut the dialog box.

> *Once a symbol occurs in the active document, double-clicking it displays the **Symbol** dialog box.*

Assigning a shortcut key to a symbol

You can use a shortcut key to insert a commonly used symbol quickly.

♦ **Insert**
  Symbol

♦ Select the symbol concerned.

♦ Click the **Shortcut Key** button.

*The insertion point flashes in the **Press new shortcut key** box.*

♦ Enter a key combination of your choice (for example ⌨Ctrl or ⌨⇧Shift pressed simultaneously with another key).

*The shortcut you have just defined is displayed in the **Current keys** box.*
*Check that **[unassigned]** appears under the heading **Currently assigned to**. In the **Description** box you can read the font and the ANSI code of the symbol, visible in the **Symbol** box.*

♦ Click **Assign** then **Close**.

❑ *To insert the symbol into the text, press the shortcut key(s) you have assigned to it.*

Inserting a page break

♦ Position the insertion point at the beginning of the line which is going to follow the page break.

♦ **Insert**
  Break

♦ Select **Page Break** and click **OK**.

> All around are scattered little coral islands. Coconut trees have grown there, like green bouquets sprouting from the sea. At the edge of the lagoon, basks **Vaitape**, the main town.
>
> ----------------------------------- Page Break -----------------------------------
>
> *A chain of coral protects it like a dike*

In Page Layout view, if the nonprinting characters are visible, a dotted line appears on the screen. This is how Word represents a page break.

❑ *To delete a page break place the insertion point on the page break line and press* Del .

Inserting a line break

By this method, you can start a new line without changing paragraph.

♦ Press ⇧ Shift ↵ .

The insertion point moves on to the next line without starting a new paragraph.

♦ If you wish, activate the display of nonprinting characters to see the line break represented:

> **Billings Boards**↵
> European·Vision·Business·Village,↵
> West·Cliff,↵
> Sussex ¶

Inserting a break between sections

A section is part of a document which has a particular layout (for example, in columns).

♦ Position the insertion point at the beginning of the new section you wish to create.

Word 98 for Macintos

♦ **Insert Break**

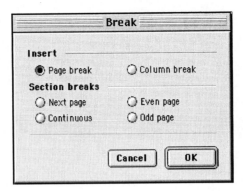

♦ In the **Section breaks** frame, choose the type of separation you want between the sections:

Next page A page break between sections.

Continuous The new section begins straight after the previous one.

Even page Word will start to print the new section on the next even-numbered page.

Odd page Word will start to print the new section on the next odd-numbered page.

♦ Click **OK**.

Inserting a hyperlink

It is possible to insert into your document a reference to another file or to a Web page.

♦ Position the insertion point where you wish to insert the link, or select the text which you are going to use as a link.

♦ **Insert Hyperlink**   ♦ K

♦ Enter the name of the file, to which the link refers, in **Link to file or URL**.

*You could also click the **Select** button then select the file.*

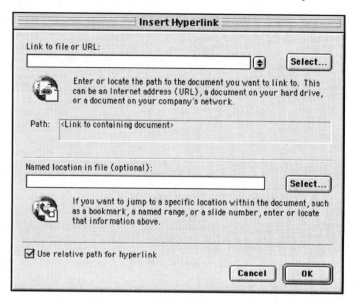

♦ If appropriate, use **Named location in file (optional)** to specify (for example) the bookmark or the range of cells that you want to reach.

♦ If you need an absolute reference in the hyperlink, deactivate **Use relative path for hyperlink**.

♦ Click **OK**.

The selected text appears in blue. If no text has been selected, the link is represented by the path to the file, which also appears in blue.

When you point the link (without clicking), the mouse pointer takes the shape of a hand and the link appears in a ScreenTip.

♦ Click the hyperlink to activate it.

The linked document and the Web toolbar appear on the screen.

♦ Click ⬅ to return to your document.

. . . . *Personal notes* . . . .

Moving/copying part of a text

♦ Select the text to be moved or copied.

♦ If you wish to move the selected text:

Edit ♦ X
Cut

♦ If you wish to copy the selected text:

Edit ♦ C
Copy

Whichever of the above you choose, the selected text is stored in a temporary memory called the clipboard.

♦ Position the insertion point where the selected text is to go.

♦ **Edit** ♦ V
Paste

The contents of the clipboard appear at the insertion point.

Moving/copying text without the clipboard

It is possible to move or copy text without first storing it in the clipboard.

♦ Select the passage.

♦ To move it press: F2 .
To copy it press: ⇧ Shift F2 .

*On the status bar, Word writes the question "**Copy to where?**".*

♦ Position the insertion point in the required place.

Note the insertion point's new form.

♦ To insert text you are moving (after use of F2), press F4 .
To insert text you are copying (after use of ⇧ Shift F2), press ↵ .

♦ Select the passage.

♦ Point to the selected text.

♦ To copy, press the ⌑ button and drag the text to its new position.
To move text, just drag it to where you want it to be.

While the file is being moved, a rectangle appears attached to the mouse pointer; if the file is being copied, the rectangle contains a + sign.

Copying formats

♦ Select the text whose format you wish to copy. If you are copying the format of a paragraph, include the end of paragraph mark in the selection.

♦ Click ⌑.

Notice the new form adopted by the mouse pointer in the workspace.

♦ Drag to select the text to which you want to apply the format. If you are formatting a paragraph, remember to select the end of paragraph mark.

❑ *If you double-click ⌑ you can select several paragraphs to format in the same way. Press* Esc *when you have selected all the paragraphs concerned.*

Printing a document	◆ Click the 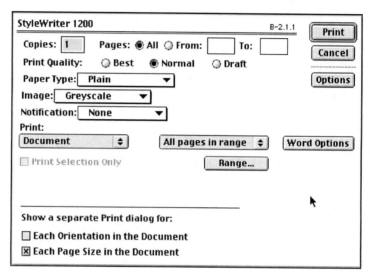 tool.

Printing should begin immediately.

Defining options for printing

Specifying which part of the text to print

◆ **File**   ◆ ⌘ P
   Print...

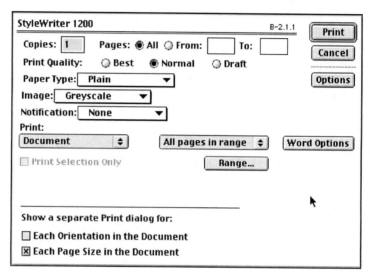

*Notice the **All** option means that by default all the document will be printed.*

◆ To print a previously selected passage click the **Print Selection Only** option.

◆ To print certain pages input the number of the first page to be printed in the **From** edit box and that of the last page to be printed in the **To** edit box.

◆ Click **Print**.

Printing several copies

♦ **File**
Print

♦ In the **Copies** box, enter the number required.

♦ If necessary, specify the range to be printed.

♦ Click **Print**.

♦ ⌘ P

**Altering
the orientation
of the page**

♦ Select the text concerned, or put the insertion point towards the top of the section to be modified.

♦ **File**
Page Setup

♦ Click the **Orientation** you require: **Portrait** or **Landscape**.

The page in the preview frame changes orientation.

♦ Use the **Apply Size and Orientation To** pop-up menu to define the passage concerned.

Whole document   The new format applies to all sections.

Selected text   A section break will be inserted before and after the selected text.

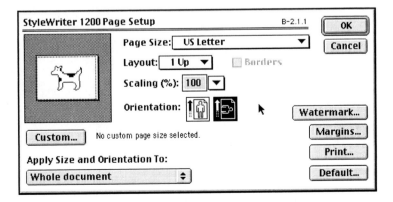

♦ Click **OK**.

❏ *When you change the page orientation, Word takes the values in place for the upper and lower margins and applies them to the left and right margins, and vice-versa.*

**Viewing
a document as
it will appear
when printed**

Displaying a Print Preview

♦ **File
Print Preview**   ♦

*An image of the document appears as Word would print it.
The percentage of magnification (zoom) applied to the page is visible on the toolbar. On the status bar, Word indicates which page you are viewing.*

♦ To see another page, use the scroll bar, or the keys Pg Up and Pg Dn.

Viewing a number of pages at once

♦ Once in Print Preview, click ▦.

♦ Drag to indicate the number of pages you wish to see, and how they should be presented.

❏ *To return to viewing a single page, click* ▢.

Zooming in on a preview

♦ Point the part of the text you wish to see close up.

The mouse pointer takes on the form of a magnifying glass containing a + sign. This indicates that the current presentation is smaller than actual size.

♦ Click the text.

The passage is presented at its actual size, and the + sign in the magnifying glass is replaced by a -.

♦ To return to the scaled-down presentation, click the document again.

Adjusting the size of a printed document

If there are just a few lines of text on the last page of a document, you may prefer Word to adjust the layout so that all the text fits into the previous pages.

♦ Click ⬛.

Displaying the rulers in Print Preview

♦ Click ⬛.

Modifying the margins from within Print Preview

♦ Once in Print Preview, display the rulers.

♦ Drag the marker along the ruler until it indicates the margin width you require.

Printing

♦ Once in Print Preview, click ⬛.

To return to the workspace

♦ Click the **Close** button, or press Esc.

Changing the margins of a document

♦ Select the text concerned, or position the insertion point towards the top of the section.

♦ **File**
Page Setup

♦ Click the **Margins** button.

*By default, Word leaves 2.5 cm margins and a **Gutter** (margin for binding) of 0 cm. For a document in which both sides of each page are printed, the left and right margins alternately are next to the binding.*

♦ Activate the check box if the document is to have **Mirror margins** (inside and outside margins of facing pages the same width).

*If you activate **Mirror margins**, you will notice that the **Left** and **Right** options are replaced by **Inside** and **Outside**, and that two pages are displayed in the preview box.*
*The **Inside** margin will be the right one of an even-numbered page, and the left one of an odd-numbered page.*
*The **Outside** margin will be the left one of an even-numbered page, and the right one of an odd-numbered page.*

♦ Modify the margins as you require.

Remember to respect the minimum margins demanded by your printer.

♦ Use the **Apply to** list to choose the part of the document for which the margins need to change.

♦ Enter.

In **Page Layout** view, the margins can be altered by moving the corresponding markers along the horizontal and vertical rulers. In this case, the new margin format applies to the section containing the insertion point.

Printing an envelope

♦ If the delivery address is already entered, select it.

♦ **Tools**
   Envelopes and Labels

♦ If necessary, activate the **Envelopes** tab.

*This is where you input the **Delivery address** and the **Return address** (Word displays the address entered when the program was installed. You have access to this via **Tools - Preferences - User Information** tab).*

♦ If the **Delivery address** has not already been selected, enter it here.

♦ If you do not need the return address to appear, check the **Omit** box.

♦ Otherwise, enter an address under **Return address**.

♦ Click the **Options** button.

♦ Under the **Envelope Options** tab:

  – enter the **Envelope size,**

  – define the details of presentation for the addresses.

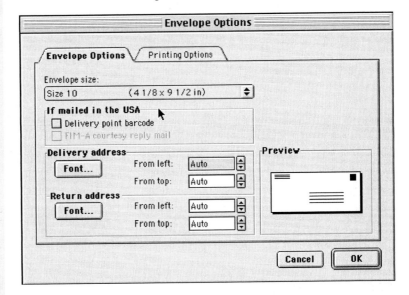

♦ In the **Printing Options** tab, choose the **Feed method** and the type of feed (check the **Use envelope feeder** box as required).

♦ Click **OK**.

♦ Choose whether to **Print** the envelope straight away or to **Add to Document**.

If you have modified the return address, Word prompts you to save.

♦ Click **Yes** if you wish the address entered to become the address by default, or click **No**.

When an envelope is added to a document, it is inserted at the top of the document as a new section; the double dotted line is visible underneath it on the screen. The new page created for the section is numbered 0.

Managing headers and footers

Headers and footers are lines of text appearing, respectively, in the upper and lower margins of a document.

Creating headers and footers

♦ Position the insertion point at the beginning of the document.

♦ **View**
   Header and Footer

Word prompts you to create a header first. The Header and Footer toolbar appears:

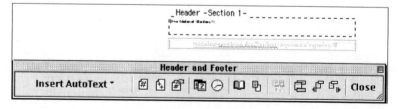

♦ To move on to creating a footer, and back again, click .

♦ Enter the content of your header/footer, and format it as you require.

Text is entered inside the dashed box.

♦ When all the text has been entered, click the **Close** button of the **Header and Footer** toolbar.

❏ *Headers and footers are visible on the screen only when the document is displayed in Page Layout view, or in Print Preview.*

❏ *Unless otherwise specified, headers are printed 1.25 cm from the top of the sheet, and footers 1.25 cm from the bottom (**File - Page Setup - Margins** button).*

❏ *If the upper and lower margins cannot contain the header/footer, Word modifies them.*

Inserting variable data into headers and footers

♦ Go into **View - Header and Footer**.

♦ Activate the presentation required.

♦ The following can be inserted:

[#]	page numbers.
[+]	the total number of pages.
[date]	the computer's control date.
[clock]	the time, as set in the computer.

Customing the format of page numbers

♦ Go into **View - Header and Footer** for the section where the page numbers should appear in a different format.

♦ Click [#].

```
┌─────────────────────────────────────────────────────┐
│░░░░░░░░░░░░░░░░ Page Number Format ░░░░░░░░░░░░░░░░░░░│
├─────────────────────────────────────────────────────┤
│                                                       │
│  Number format:              │ 1, 2, 3, ...  │ ▲▼│   │
│  ☐ Include chapter number                             │
│     Chapter starts with style  │ Heading 1    │ ▲▼│  │
│     Use separator:             │ - (hyphen)   │ ▲▼│  │
│     Examples:  1-1, 1-A                               │
│  Page numbering                                       │
│     ⦿ Continue from previous section                  │
│     ○ Start at:          │          │ ▲▼              │
│                    ▲                                   │
│                                                       │
│                        ┌──────────┐ ┌──────────┐      │
│                        │  Cancel  │ │    OK    │      │
│                        └──────────┘ └──────────┘      │
└─────────────────────────────────────────────────────┘
```

♦ Modify the options.

♦ Click **OK**.

❏ *You could also stay in the text and change the format of the page numbers: position the insertion point at the beginning of the section and use* ***Insert - Page Numbers - Format.***

Using a different header/footer

♦ Position the insertion point in the section requiring a header/footer different from the preceding ones.

♦ **View**
Header and Footer

♦ Click the 🔲 tool to deactivate it, breaking the link between the header used for previous sections and the one for the current and following sections.

♦ Give the new header/footer.

♦ Enter the modifications by clicking the **Close** button.

Defining a header/footer for the first page

♦ Position the insertion point at the beginning of the document.

♦ **View**
  Header and Footer

♦ Click .

♦ If necessary, activate the **Layout** tab.

♦ In the **Headers and Footers** frame, activate the choice **Different first page**.

♦ Click **OK**.

♦ Give the header/footer for the first page.

Using different headers/footers for odd-/even- pages

♦ **View**
  Header and Footer

♦ Click .

♦ Under the **Layout** tab, activate the choice **Different odd and even**.

♦ Click **OK**.

♦ Enter the header/footer of the even-numbered pages, then click 🔲 to enter the header/footer for the odd-numbered pages.

> *To create a watermark, insert a picture while you are creating the header or footer, click* 🔲 *, then size the picture and set the wrapping options to define how the picture relates to the text.*

Formatting characters

Characters can be put into bold type, italics...

♦ If you have already entered the characters concerned, select them.

♦ Click one or more of the buttons on the **Formatting** bar to apply the attribute you require :

B	**Bold** type
I	*Italics*
U	Underlined

The buttons you have used appear pressed in, and the characters are written in the format you have chosen.

♦ Use the following key combinations to apply the attributes you require. If you have already entered the characters concerned select then:

⌃ ⌘ **B**	**Bold**
⌃ ⌘ **I**	*Italic*
⌃ ⌘ **U**	Underlined
⌃ ⌘ ⇧Shift **D**	Double Underlined
⌃ ⌘ ⇧Shift **W**	Words only Underlined
⌃ ⌘ ⇧Shift **K**	SMALL CAPITALS
⌃ ⌘ ⇧Shift **A**	CAPITALS
⌃ ⌘ ⇧Shift **+**	in Superscript
⌃ ⌘ **=**	in Subscript
⌃ ⌘ ⇧Shift **H**	Hidden text

❏ *To put characters into superscript, you must use the + key on the main (alphanumerical) keyboard.*

♦ If you have already entered the characters concerned, select them.

♦ **Format**　　　　　　　　　　　　♦ ⌃ ⌘ **D**
　Font

♦ If necessary, activate the **Font** tab.

♦ Make your choice from the **Font style** list, the **Underline** pop-up menu, and the **Effects** frame.

*In the **Preview** box, Word shows the text selected in the format chosen.*

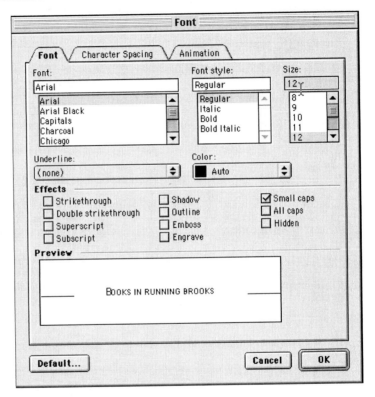

♦ Click **OK**.

Cancelling character formats

♦ If the text is already entered, select it.

♦ To cancel a format, click the same button or press the same keys that you used to activate it.
To cancel all formats at once, press ⌘ ⇧ Shift **Z**.

❏*Using the same format button/keys twice activates then deactivates the format.*

Changing the font and the size of characters

♦ If the text is already entered, select the characters concerned.

♦ On the **Formatting** toolbar, open the list box containing font sizes (in points), or the fonts list.

Word produces a list of sizes available for the font you are using, or a list of fonts.

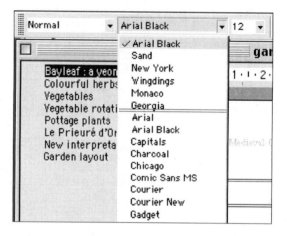

Word puts the last 6 fonts used at the top of the font list.

♦ Click the required font and/or size.

> You can also change the font and/or the size of characters by *Format - Font*, *Font* tab.

Modifying the space between characters

♦ If necessary, select the characters concerned.

♦ **Format**   ♦ ⌘ D
  Font

♦ Activate the **Character Spacing** tab, then open the **Spacing** popup menu.

◆ Activate the spacing you require:

Expanded   more space between characters.

Condensed   less space between characters.

◆ You can also enter the exact space to be left between characters, expressed as a number of points. Do this in the **By** box.

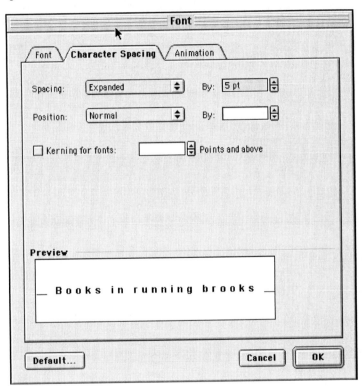

◆ Click **OK**.

Colouring or highlighting characters

♦ Select the characters concerned.

♦ Open the appropriate list by clicking its down arrow:

 to change the colour of the characters.

 to highlight them with a band of colour.

♦ Click the colour you prefer.

> To apply the last colour selected, simply click the tool button or without opening the list.

Applying an animation effect

♦ Select the characters concerned.

♦ **Format**
  Font
  Animation tab

♦ ⌘ D

♦ Choose the effect you require.

Applying a border to characters

♦ Select the characters concerned.

♦ On the **Table and Borders** toolbar, choose a style, a line weight and a colour for the border.

♦ Click .

Changing the standard presentation of characters

You can change the default font, style, attributes, spacing...

♦ Whatever the position of the insertion point, define the new standard presentation via the menu **Format - Font, Font** tab.

*This can be done only via the menu, as there is no other way to the **Default** command button.*

♦ Click the **Default** button:

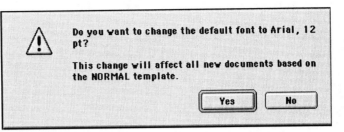

Word displays the choice just made, and reminds you that, if you go ahead, the template on which the document is based will be modified.

♦ Confirm by the **Yes** button.

All characters adopt the new standard presentation, except for those that have previously been modified specifically to be different from the new standard presentation.

. . . . *Personal notes* . . . .

Standard presentation of paragraphs

◆ To change the standard style used for paragraphs, modify the style called **Normal**.

◆ To return a paragraph to the presentation defined in the style, select it then press ⌘ ⇥ **Q**.

Setting a tab

Here are the different types of tab, and the effects they produce.

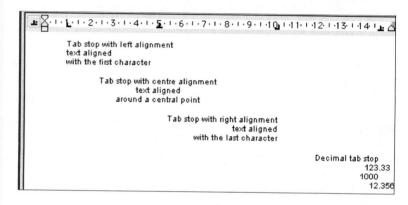

◆ Select the paragraphs concerned, or position the insertion point inside the paragraph.

◆ Activate the type of tab required, by clicking once or several times on the button to the left of the ruler:

L	left tab
⊥	centre tab
⌐	right tab
⊥	decimal tab

◆ Click the mark on the ruler corresponding to the position you intend for the tab.

The tab stop appears on the ruler.

♦ **Format**
  Tabs

♦ For each tab you wish to set:

   – enter the position in **Tab stop position**,

   – choose the **Alignment**,

   – define the **Leader** line,

   – click the **Set** button.

*Each tab stop you set in this way appears in the list of existing tabs (**Tab stop position**).*

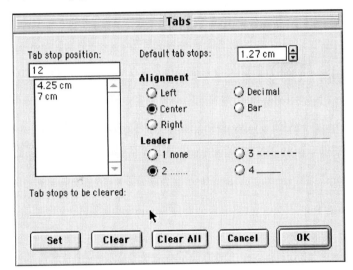

♦ When all the tab stops are set, click **OK**.

The tab stops are displayed on the ruler.

❏ *By this menu, you can change the position of **Default tab stops** (originally set every 1.25 cm).*

❏ *When you set a personal tab, Word deletes any default tab stops situated in front of it.*

*Once a personal tab is displayed on the ruler, just double-click it to activate the **Tabs** dialog box from the **Format** menu.*

Managing existing tabs

♦ To <u>move</u> a tab stop, drag its marker to a new position.

♦ To <u>delete</u> a tab stop, drag its marker right off the ruler.

As soon as the marker has crossed the top or bottom line of the ruler, it disappears.

*If you need to cancel all your personal tabs, the quickest way is to go into the **Tabs** dialog box, and activate the **Clear All** button followed by **OK**.*

Indentation of paragraphs

These examples show the effect of the four types of indent proposed on the presentation of paragraphs.

> **Left Indentation**: here is a paragraph with a 5cm indentation from the left margin.
>
> **Right Indentation**: here is a paragraph with the right indentation marker positioned at 7cm.
>
> **Indentation of the first line**: here is a paragraph in which only the first line has a 3cm indentation from the left margin.
>
> **Hanging indentation of the first line**: here is a paragraph whose first line has a –3cm indentation from the left margin.

♦ Select the paragraphs concerned, or position the insertion point in the paragraph.

On the ruler there are four indentation markers, corresponding to the four types of indent:

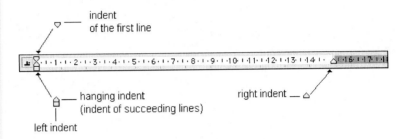

♦ Drag the markers to the required position.

While the mouse button is held down, you see a vertical line; as soon as you release it, the indent you have defined is taken into account.

❏ *If you move the left indent marker, the first line indent and hanging indent markers move as well.*

You can also use the ⊟ *and* ⊟ *buttons to move the left indent to the next tab stop, or the preceding one.*

♦ It the text is already entered, select it.

♦ **Format**　　　　　　Double-click one of
　Paragraph　　　　the four indentation markers
　Indents and Spacing tab

PARAGRAPHS

Paragraph dialog box showing Indents and Spacing tab:

- Alignment: Left
- Outline level: Body text
- **Indentation**
  - Left: 0 cm
  - Right: 0 cm
  - Special: (none)
  - By:
- **Spacing**
  - Before: 0 pt
  - After: 0 pt
  - Line spacing: Single
  - At:
- **Preview**
- Tabs... Cancel OK

*In this dialog box, the **Indentation** frame offers the choice between **Left** and **Right** and between first line and hanging indentation (available in the **Special** pop-up menu).*

♦ Enter the value of the indent, in the specified measurement units.

*To obtain an "outdent" of the first line, choose **Hanging** in the **Special** pop-up menu.*

♦ Click **OK**.

❑ *By default, the text boxes propose values in centimetres. If you prefer to use another unit of measurement, enter a value followed by: **pt** for points, " for inches, **cm** for centimetres, **pi** for picas.*

To change the unit by default, go into **Tools - Preferences - General** tab and choose the **Measurement units** you require. The ruler of the active document appears in the unit you have specified.

66

♦ If you wish, activate **Tab and backspace set left indent** under the **Edit** tab of the **Tools - Preferences** dialog box.

♦ Once this option is active, use the ⬚ key to increase the indent from the left, or use ⬚ to decrease it.

Entering text in the left margin

You can put paragraphs in the left margin without modifying the document's margins.

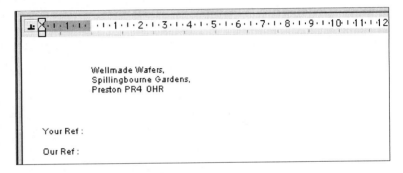

♦ Select the text if it is already entered.

♦ Drag the left indent marker to the left.

Note that it is impossible to make a negative indentation greater than the width of the left margin.

Creating a hanging indent of the first line

A hanging indent of the first line is useful for the following type of presentation:

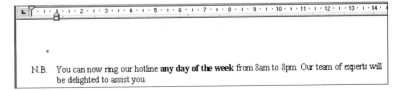

♦ If the text is already entered, select it, otherwise place the insertion point where you require this style of presentation.

♦ On the ruler, move the hanging indent marker towards the right.

❑ *You can use the **Paragraph** option in the **Format** menu to obtain the same effect. Choose **Hanging** in the **Special** pop-up menu, and enter the value in the **By** box.*

Modifying the alignment of paragraphs

♦ If the texts are already entered, select them.

♦ According to the alignment you require, use one of the following techniques:

Alignment		
Left	▤	⌃ ⌘ L
Centred	▤	⌃ ⌘ E
Right	▤	⌃ ⌘ R
Justified	▤	⌃ ⌘ J

❑ *These alignments are also accessible by **Format - Paragraph**, **Indents and Spacing** tab.*

Modifying the line spacing

Line spacing is the space between lines in a paragraph. By default, it is calculated according to the size of the characters in the paragraph.

♦ Select the text to be formatted, if it is already entered.

♦ **Format**   Double-click one of
  Paragraph   the four indentation markers
  Indents and Spacing tab

♦ Open the **Line spacing** pop-up menu; Word offers three standard spacing values **Single**, **1,5 lines**, **Double** and three other options:

At least	minimum value of line spacing (enter the value in the **At:** box).
Exactly	the value remains fixed: Word cannot alter it whatever the size of the characters (enter the value in the **At:** box).
Multiple	each line is spaced according to its tallest character.

♦ Click the new line-spacing option.

♦ If necessary, enter a precise value in the **At** box.

♦ Click **OK**.

Modifying the spacing of paragraphs	*You can unpack your text without having to insert blank lines, by leaving space before and/or after paragraphs.*

♦ If necessary select the text concerned.

♦ **Format**   Double-click one of
  Paragraph   the four indentation markers
  Indents and Spacing tab

♦ Under **Spacing**, define the value of space to be left **Before** and/or **After** a paragraph (use the unit of measurement you prefer: see below).

```
┌─────────────────────────────────────────────────────────────┐
│                          Paragraph                           │
│ ┌─────────────────────┐┌──────────────────────┐             │
│ │ Indents and Spacing ││  Line and Page Breaks │             │
│                                                              │
│  Alignment:     [ Justified  ◆]    Outline level:  [Body text ◆]│
│  Indentation                                                 │
│     Left:       [0 cm      ▲▼]                               │
│                                    Special:         By:      │
│     Right:      [0 cm      ▲▼]     [(none)   ◆]   [       ▲▼]│
│                                                              │
│  Spacing                                                     │
│     Before:     [18 pt     ▲▼]                               │
│                                    Line spacing:    At:      │
│     After:      [12 pt     ▲▼]     [Single   ◆]   [       ▲▼]│
│                                                              │
│  Preview                                                     │
│   ┌────────────────────────────────────────────────────┐    │
│   │                                                    │    │
│   │                                                    │    │
│   │                                                    │    │
│   └────────────────────────────────────────────────────┘    │
│                                                              │
│  [ Tabs... ]                           [ Cancel ]  [  OK  ]  │
└─────────────────────────────────────────────────────────────┘
```

♦ Click **OK**.

❑ *By default, these text boxes propose values in points. Here too, you can use a different unit of measurement providing you indicate, after the value, **cm** for centimetres, **li** for lines, " for inches, **pi** for picas.*

If you prefer to work from the keyboard, press ⌃ ⌘ **0** *(zero, on the alphanumerical keyboard) to leave a blank line (12 pt) above each selected paragraph.*

**Preventing
a break
within/between
paragraphs**

Page breaks or column breaks are often undesirable in the middle of a paragraph, or between complementary paragraphs.

♦ If the page/column break is to be avoided within a paragraph, select that paragraph; if it is to be prevented between two paragraphs, select the first; if it is to be prevented between several paragraphs, select all except the last.

◆ **Format
Paragraph**

Double-click one of
the four indentation marks

◆ Activate the **Line and Page Breaks** tab.

◆ To avoid a page/column break within a paragraph, activate the choice **Keep lines together**; to avoid a page/column break between paragraphs choose **Keep with next**.

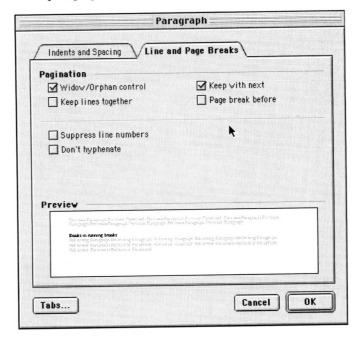

◆ Click **OK**.

**Putting a border
around
a paragraph**

◆ Click the paragraph concerned, or if there are several paragraphs, select them.

◆ Display the **Tables and Borders** toolbar by clicking [image].

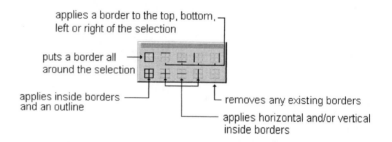

♦ In this bar's first list, choose the line style for the border.

♦ In the second list, choose the border line thickness.

♦ Click 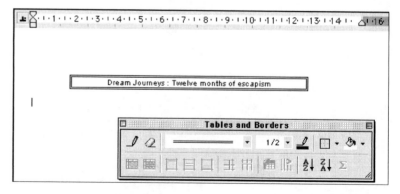 to choose a colour for the border.

♦ Open the ⬚▾ list and select the type of border you wish to apply:

applies a border to the top, bottom, left or right of the selection

puts a border all around the selection

applies inside borders and an outline

removes any existing borders

applies horizontal and/or vertical inside borders

The border extends from the left indent to the right indent.

Dream Journeys : Twelve months of escapism

♦ To change the width of the border, change the left indent and/or the right indent.

❑ *Borders are also accessible via* **Format - Borders and Shading**.

**Modifying
the space
between the text
and the border**

♦ Select the paragraphs concerned.

♦ **Format
Borders and Shading
Borders** tab

♦ Click the **Options** button.

♦ In the **From text** boxes enter the values of the spaces between the text and the border.

♦ Click **OK**.

❏ *Once again, the unit of measurement proposed (the point) can be altered by entering cm, pi or " after the value.*

❏ *The space between the border and the text cannot exceed 31 points.*

**Shading
a paragraph**

You can highlight a paragraph by setting it on a coloured background.

♦ Select the paragraphs concerned.

♦ If necessary, display the **Tables and Borders** toolbar by clicking [image].

♦ Choose the shading from the [image] list.

❏ *Applying a coloured background to a paragraph tends to affect the legibility of the text: take care when choosing colours, style and the size of characters.*

♦ Select the paragraphs concerned.

♦ **Format
Borders and Shading
Shading** tab

♦ In **Fill**, indicate the background colour you require.

♦ In **Style**, indicate the density of the pattern you want to apply over the fill colour.

♦ Choose a colour for the pattern from the **Color** list.

♦ Click **OK**.

. . . . *Personal notes* . . . .

**Applying
a border
to a page**

♦ Position the insertion point in the section concerned.

♦ **Format
Borders and Shading
Page Border** tab

♦ Under **Setting**, choose the type of border you require: **Box, Shadow, 3-D, Custom.**

*The **Custom** option applies a different style of border to each side of the page.*

♦ Choose the **Style** and **Color** of the border, or if you prefer, choose a pattern from the **Art** list.

♦ If necessary, modify the **Width** of the border.

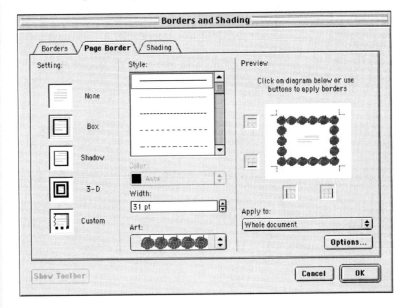

♦ In the **Apply to** list, choose the part of the document to which you want to apply the border.

♦ Click **OK.**

**Applying
a background**

*A background applies to an entire document. Although you can see
the background on the screen, you cannot print it.*

♦ **Format
Background**

♦ Choose a colour for the background
or
create a custom colour, in **More Colors**, **Custom** tab
or
apply a texture, gradient, pattern or picture.

Using a graphic effect as a background

♦ Activate the **Fill Effects** option.

♦ According to the background you have in mind, choose the **Gradient** tab, the **Texture** tab the **Pattern** tab or the **Picture** tab.

♦ Set the options, then click **OK**.

**Creating
a Drop Cap**

A drop cap is an illuminated initial, opening a chapter or paragraph.

♦ Select and format the future drop cap (font and size of character).

♦ **Format
Drop Cap...**

♦ Under **Position**, choose the effect you prefer.

♦ Customise the presentation by changing the **Font**, the number of lines taken up by the drop cap (in **Lines to drop**), and the **Distance from text**.

Drop Cap

Position

None   Dropped   In Margin

Options

Font:

Arial

Lines to drop: 3

Distance from text: 0 cm

Cancel   OK

♦ Click **OK**.

The drop cap is created in a frame represented by a grey outline.

Numbering and Bullets

Two options are proposed on the toolbar, but other choices are accessible via the menu.

♦ Select the paragraphs you wish to format, if they are already entered.

♦ Click ⊞ to number the selected paragraphs.

Click ⊞ to put a bullet before each paragraph.

Example

Conclusions

• The experiment at Bayleaf shows how self-sufficient the yeoman homestead was in the days before seed shops, timber merchants or garden centres. It also demonstrates just how colourful a kitchen garden was at this level of society, when gardens lacked herbaceous *borders*

• With the use of animal manure, friendly insects for the biological control of pests, and employing a ground-covering "mulch" and green manure, it was a wholly organic method of gardening.

◆ Enter the paragraphs and select them.

◆ **Format**
Bullets and Numbering

◆ Click the tab dealing with the type of list you wish to create: **Bulleted** or **Numbered**.

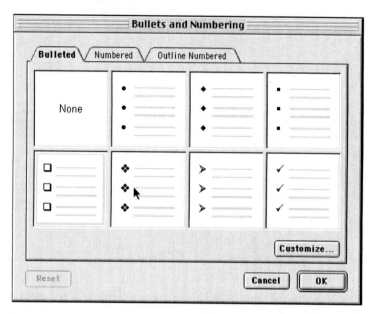

◆ Click the model you prefer, or use the **Customize** button to create something different.

◆ Click **OK**.

Presenting text in columns

◆ **Format**
Columns

◆ Under **Presets**, choose the basic presentation you require.

♦ Indicate whether or not all the columns are to be of identical width, using the **Equal column width** check box.

♦ If necessary, change the **Width** value and the **Spacing** (the space left between columns) value for each column.

♦ Check the box to draw a **Line between** the columns.

♦ Use the **Apply to** pop-up menu to define the part of the text to be presented in columns.

♦ Click **OK**.

❑ In **Normal** view, only one column of text can be seen. To view the presentation in columns, you must be in **Page Layout** view.

❑ The [⊞] tool may be used but, in this case, you can neither define the width of the columns, nor draw a line between them.

Inserting a column break

♦ Place the insertion point at the beginning of the line which is to follow the column break.

♦ **Insert**
Break
Column break

♦

❏ *When the non-printing characters are displayed, a dotted line and the words **Column Break** indicate the position of the break.*

. . . . *Personal notes* . . . .

**Inserting
a picture,
sound or video
from the gallery**

♦ Put the insertion point where you wish to position the picture, sound or video.

♦ **Insert
Picture
Clip Art**

♦ Click the tab dealing with the object which you want to insert.

♦ Select the category which contains the object.

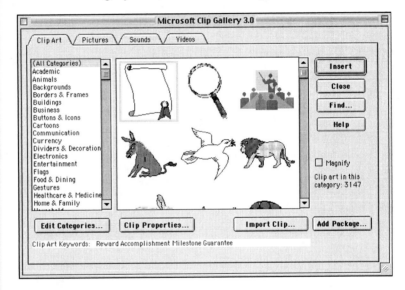

*The **Magnify** option allows you to zoom in the selected picture.*

♦ Double-click the object.

Sizing a picture which you have inserted

♦ Click the inserted picture.

Selection handles appear around it.

♦ To resize the picture without distorting it, drag one of the corner handles.
To distort a picture, drag a handle in the middle of one of the sides.

◆ To crop the picture, click on the **Picture** toolbar and drag one of the handles to reduce the visible area of the picture.

 *In the **Format - Picture** dialog box, you can give an exact size for the picture. The **Reset** button returns the picture to its original size.*

Drawing a shape

◆ Display the **Drawing** toolbar.

Drawing a simple shape

◆ Click the tool corresponding to the object you wish to draw:

   line

   arrow

   rectangle

ellipse

When the mouse pointer is in the workspace, it takes the form of a black cross hair.

◆ Hold the mouse button down, and draw the object with the pointer.

❑ *To draw an ellipse, drag as if you were drawing a rectangle of a similar size.*

 To obtain a perfect square or circle, hold down the ⇧ Shift key while drawing with the rectangle/ellipse tool.
To draw a rectangle/square or an ellipse/circle beginning in the centre rather than from an edge, hold the ⌗ key down while you are drawing.

Drawing an AutoShape

◆ Open the **AutoShapes** list on the **Drawing** toolbar.

◆ Activate the category which contains the shape, then select it.

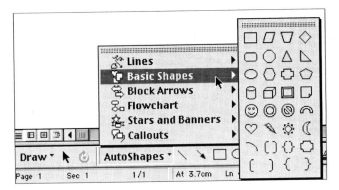

◆ Drag to draw the shape.

Inserting a WordArt text effect

This application enables you to introduce special typographic effects into your text:

◆ Position the insertion point where you would like to use the characters.

◆ Click the ⊿ button on the **Drawing** toolbar.

◆ Choose the effect you wish to apply.

♦ Click **OK**.

♦ Type in your text, using ⏎ to change line.

♦ Format the text, using the **Font** and **Font Size** lists and the ▣**B**
and ▣**I** buttons.

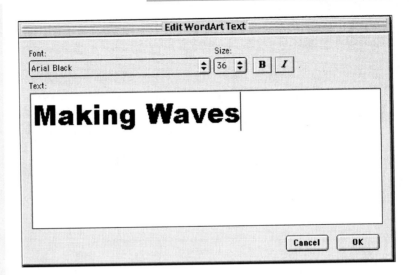

♦ Click **OK**.

The text appears as an object in the document; the **WordArt** *toolbar is displayed.*

♦ To remove the selection from the object, click elsewhere in the document.

Editing WordArt text

♦ Click the WordArt object to select it.

♦ Use the buttons on the **WordArt** toolbar to edit it.

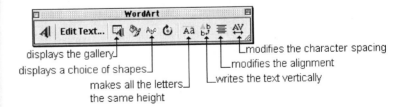

Clicking the **Edit Text** *button displays the dialog box used for entering text.*

Creating a text box

Creating a text box allows you to position text anywhere on the page, or to put paragraphs side by side.

Example:

> SIXTY THOUSAND or more cavalrymen, along with bombardiers to work the mangonels, the giant catapults of siege warfare, started westward from Mongolia in 1236. A few months later, this force reached the Volga river near today's Russian city of Kazan.
>
> Today a dam at Kazak makes a lake so wide I can't see the opposite bank. In fact, for most of its length Mother Volga is a series of stair-step reservoirs.
>
> Beside the river - free-flowing then, of course - the Mongol horsemen fell upon the capital of the kingdom of Bulgar. It's rulers, kings of the
>
> *And who, brothers, fathers, and children, seeing this, God's infliction on the whole Russian Land, does not lament?*
> *- CHRONICLE OF NOVGOROD*
>
> city rode out to parley with the invaders. What tribute would the Mongols accept for sparing Ryazan? They demanded "a tenth of everything," even a tenth of the women and children, according to the *Chronicle of Novgorod*. "Only when none of us remain," the nobles answered defiantly. So the Mongols cut trees and surrounded Ryazan's walls with a stockade. Shielded from the defender's arrows, mangonel crews bombarded the city with stones for five days. Then the Mongols poured in, engaging in an orgy of rape and pillage.

♦ Click ▤ on the **Drawing** toolbar.

♦ Drag to draw the text box.

♦ Enter your text like an ordinary paragraph.

♦ Click outside the box to end.

❏ *Text in a text box can be formatted using the usual commands.*

❏ *If the text is too long to fit in the text box, you will not be able to see all of it.*

Creating a link between two text boxes

You can use a linked text box to take the overflow if one box cannot hold all the text.

♦ Create the first text box and enter the text.

♦ Create a second text box, but leave it empty.

♦ Select the first text box.

♦ Open the shortcut menu (press Ctrl and click one edge of the box) and choose **Create Text Box Link**.

The mouse pointer changes shape.

♦ Click the empty text box.

The excess text from the first text box is transferred to the second.

. . . . *Personal notes* . . . .

Selecting objects

♦ If necessary, click ⬚ on the **Drawing** toolbar.

♦ <u>For one object</u>: click in the object you wish to select. If the object is not filled, click its outline.

♦ <u>For several objects</u>: select the first, then the others by holding down ⌹Shift while clicking.
Alternatively, drag to select the objects. In this case, be careful: an object will not be selected unless it is entirely inside the selection frame.

♦ To cancel a selection, click an empty space.

Sizing an object

♦ Select the object whose dimensions you wish to modify.

♦ Drag one of the selection handles.

❑ *If you are working with a perfect circle, square... and do not wish to distort it, hold down the* ⌹Shift *key as you drag.*

Moving an object

♦ Select the object.

♦ Point to one of its edges. When the pointer takes the form of four arrows, click and drag the shape to move it.

❑ *If the* **Snap to Grid** *option is active in* **Draw - Grid**, *the selected object can be moved only along the invisible gridlines.*

Wrapping an object

♦ Select the picture, text box or other object concerned.

♦ In the shortcut menu associated with the object (obtained by pressing ⌃Ctrl and clicking the object), choose the **Format...** option. If necessary, click the **Wrapping** tab.

♦ Choose a **Wrapping style.**

♦ In the **Wrap to** frame, indicate the effect you have in mind.

♦ If you wish, specify the **Distance from text** with reference to the edge of the object.

♦ Click **OK.**

Attaching a caption to an object

♦ Select the object concerned (picture, chart, table...).

♦ **Insert**
   Caption

♦ In the **Label** box, choose a suitable caption for the type of object: **Equation, Figure** or **Table.** Alternatively click the **New Label** button to write your own caption.

*If you choose this last option, the new text is displayed immediately in the **Caption** box.*

♦ If necessary, use the **Caption** box to add the rest of the text you wish to see.

♦ In the **Position** list, choose where the caption should go: **Above** or **Below selected item**.

♦ Click the **Numbering** button, and use the **Format** list box to specify the format of the numbers.

♦ Click **OK**.

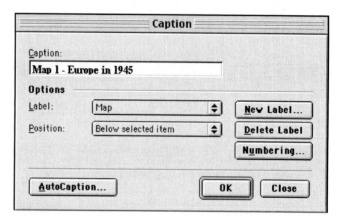

♦ Click **OK** once more to insert the caption.

❑ *The **AutoCaption** button in this dialog box is used to add captions automatically, as objects of a given type are inserted. This choice must be made at the creation of the document, before the first object has been inserted.*

Aligning objects

♦ To align objects relative to the page, open the **Draw** list on the **Drawing** toolbar, activate **Align or Distribute** and then activate the **Relative to Page** option.

If you do not activate this option the objects will be aligned relative to each other.

♦ Select the objects you wish to align.

♦ Open the **Draw** list then **Align or Distribute**.

♦ Choose the type of alignment you require.

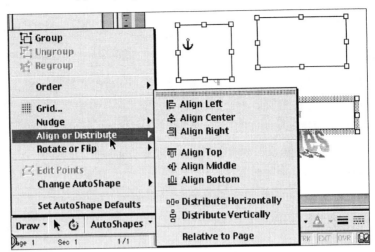

Reorganising overlapping objects

♦ Select the object that you want to move forward or send further back.

♦ Open the **Draw** list on the **Drawing** toolbar, then point to the **Order** option.

♦ Choose **Bring to Front** or **Send to Back** if you wish the selected object to be the first or last of all. Choose **Bring Forward** or **Bring Backward** to move the object forward or back one place.

Grouping/ ungrouping objects

You can group several objects (so that they can be moved all at once, for example), and ungroup them.

♦ Select the objects.

♦ Open the **Draw** list on the **Drawing** toolbar.

♦ Activate **Group** or **Ungroup**.

*The **Regroup** option regroups objects which have been ungrouped.*

**Rounding
the corners
of a rectangle**

♦ Select the rectangle concerned.

♦ Open the **Draw** list on the **Drawing** toolbar.

♦ Activate the **Change AutoShape** option.

♦ In the **Basic Shapes** list, choose the rectangle with rounded corners.

**Rotating or
flipping an object**

♦ Select the object.

Rotating an object

♦ Click .

♦ Drag one of the object's selection handles, and pivot the object as you require.

♦ When you have finished, click again.

Flipping an object, or rotating through 90°

♦ Open the **Draw** list and activate **Rotate or Flip**.

♦ Choose **Rotate Left**, **Rotate Right**, **Flip Horizontal** or **Flip Vertical**.

**Modifying
the outline
of an object**

♦ Select the object.

♦ Click one of the following buttons:

    To change the colour of the outline, or to choose a repeated pattern to replace the line.

   To change the line style (the thickness in particular).

   To change the type of line.

Colouring an object or applying a texture

♦ Select the object concerned.

♦ Click the arrow on 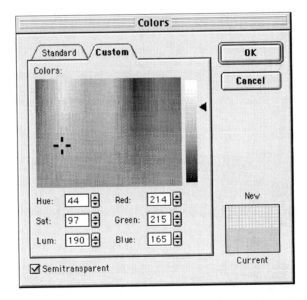.

♦ Choose the colour you wish to apply.

Customising a colour

♦ Click the arrow on ⬛ ▾ then the **More Fill Colors** option.

♦ Under the **Standard** tab, click the colour that you wish to modify.

♦ Under the **Custom** tab, move the pointer over the range of colours, varying the **Hue**, **Sat** (Saturation), **Lum** (Luminosity) of the colour and the percentage of **Red**, **Green** and **Blue** it contains.

*If the **Semitransparent** option is active, the colour will be partially transparent.*

♦ Click **OK**.

Applying a graphic effect

♦ Open 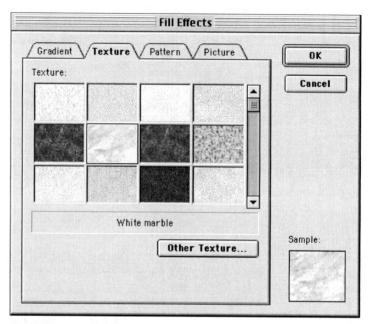 then click **Fill Effects**.

♦ Open one of the following pages:

Gradient   shades the object horizontally, vertically or diago-nally, starting from the top, bottom, corner or centre. One or two colours, or a pre-set multico-lour combination, can be used for shading.

Texture   applies a textured fill.

Pattern   applies a **Pattern**: you select **Foreground** and **Background** colours.

Picture   fills the shape with a picture.

**Giving
a shadow
to an object**

♦ Select the object.

♦ Click 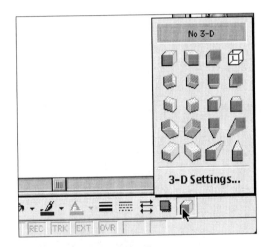.

♦ Choose the shadow effect you require.

*The **Shadow Settings** option allows you to customise the shadow (for example, you can change its colour).*

**Applying
a 3D effect**

♦ Select the object.

♦ Click .

♦ Choose the 3D effect you require.

*The **No 3-D** option allows you to return to the original shape; the **3-D Settings** option allows you to customise the effect.*

Creating a document template

A document template allows you to automate your work by saving and reusing styles of presentation and/or text.

♦ **File**
New...

You cannot use the *button on the toolbar, nor the shortcut key* ⌘ N*, because these methods do not display the dialog box.*

♦ Click the **Template** option under **Create New**.

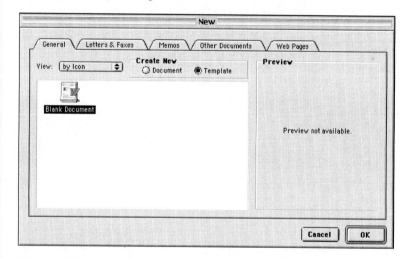

♦ Click **OK**.

The title bar tells you that you are creating a new template.

Creating a template based on another

♦ **File**
New

♦ ⌘ N

♦ Select the name of the template on which to base the new one.

♦ In the **Create New** frame, click **Template**.

♦ Click **OK**.

Saving a document template

♦ The same principles apply as for saving a document, but the template file must be stored in the **Templates** folder (or one of its subfolders), situated in the folder where Word 98 is installed.

Creating a document based on a template

Once you have created a template you can create documents incorporating the styles (or the text) it contains.

♦ **File**
New...

*Under the **General** tab, the pre-selected icon **Blank Document** allows you to create a new blank document based on the **Normal** template.*

♦ Click the tab where the template you want to use appears.

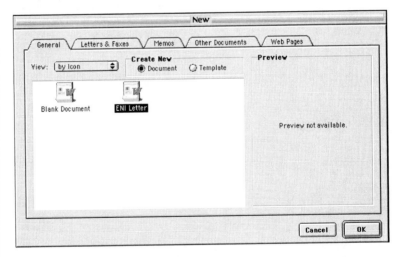

♦ Double-click the name of the template you wish to use.

A new document appears. There is nothing to indicate whether it is based on a different template from Normal.

**Opening
a document
template**

You need to open a template if you want to make changes in it.

♦ **File
Open...**

♦ O

♦ Activate the folder where the templates are stored (by default, the **Templates** folder).

♦ Open the **List Files of Type** pop-up menu and click **Document Templates**.

The display of documents is replaced by a display of templates:

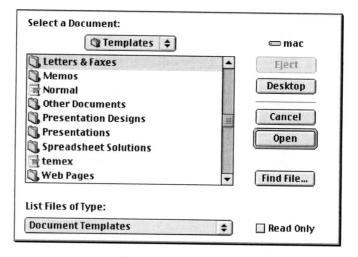

♦ Double-click the name of the document template to open.

❏ *The next time you want to open a document, remember to choose **Word Documents** in the **List Files of Type** pop-up menu.*

**Transforming
a document into
a template**

♦ Delete everything in the document that does not need to be reproduced automatically by the template.

♦ **File
Save As**

♦ Open the **Save File as Type** pop-up menu and click **Document Template**.

*Word proposes to store the file in the **Templates** folder.*

♦ If necessary, modify the name of the file in the **Save Current Document as** box.

♦ Click **Save**.

Linking another template to an existing document

This technique enables you to use the styles of a template other than the one you have used to create the active document.

♦ **Tools**
Templates and Add-Ins

♦ Click the **Attach** button under **Document template**.

The list of all the template files is displayed.

♦ Double-click the name of the template to use.

♦ Activate the choice **Automatically update document styles**.

♦ Click **OK**.

Using a Wizard (eg. for a CV)

A Wizard does automatic formatting for you. Word provides Wizards for the creation of letters, tables, certificates, bulletins...

♦ **File**
New

♦ Select the tab containing the template you require.

♦ Select the relevant template marked "Wizard" (for a CV, choose the **Resume Wizard** under the **Other Documents** tab).

♦ Click **OK**.

*Word creates a new document, and after a few moments the **Resume Wizard** dialog box is displayed. You create this new document step by step, following Word's instructions. Word does the formatting.*

♦ Click **Next** to start then choose the **Style** of CV you require.

♦ Click **Next** to go on to the next step then give the **Type** of CV.

♦ Click **Next** and fill in the **Name, Address, Phone**...

♦ Click **Next** to go on from step to step, or **Back** to return to the preceding step.

♦ Click the **Finish** button.

❑ *If you choose to save a Web page created using the Web Page Wizard, Word offers to save the file in **HTML Document** format.*

. . . . *Personal notes* . . . .

Planning styles

In a style, several elements of formatting are saved together so that they can be applied simultaneously.

Deciding where you need to use the style

♦ If you create a style in a document, you will be able to use it only in that document.

♦ If the style might be useful for other documents you create in the future, create it in the **template**.

Preparing styles

♦ On a sheet of paper, list the different types of paragraph that you use repeatedly and make a note of the formatting that you habitually apply to them.

♦ Give a name to each style of paragraph, and if you wish, associate each of these styles with a shortcut key.

The following table is an example of how you might prepare styles to use in letters.

Paragraph concerned	Formats to apply	Name of style	Shortcut key
Addresses	left indent 8 cm	ADDRESS	Ctrl 1
Reference code /Re paragraph	left indent 1.5 cm tab stop at 1.5 cm	REF/RE	Ctrl 2
Main body of letter	1st line indent 2 cm justified alignment	BODY	Ctrl 3

Creating a style

Based on existing formatting

♦ Do the formatting which is to be included in the style.

♦ Click the name of the active style in the **Styles** list box on the **Formatting** toolbar.

♦ Type the name of the new style and press ⏎.

The style is immediately applied to the current paragraph.

❏ *This technique does not allow you to define a shortcut key.*

Without existing formatting

♦ **Format**
Style

♦ For each new style created:

- Click the **New** button and give a name for the style.

- If you wish, click the **Shortcut Key** button and press the shortcut key combination which you want to associate with the style.

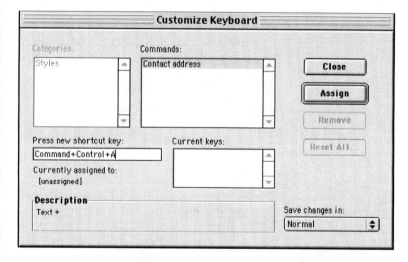

- Check that **[unassigned]** appears under **Currently assigned to**, click **Assign** then **Close**.

- Using the **Format** button, define all the formatting included in the style.

- If you are not in the template, but you want the style to be created in the template and not just in the current document, activate **Add to template**.

- Activate **Automatically update**, if you intend changes which you make in a paragraph associated with the style to affect the style itself.

- When you have finished, click **OK**.

♦ Once you have created all the styles, click **Close**.

Using a style   *There are two methods of applying a style to a text.*

♦ If necessary, select the text concerned by the style.

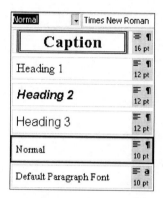

♦ Open the **Style** list box and click the name of the style you wish to use.

The formatting saved in the style is applied immediately.

♦ If necessary, select the text.

♦ Press the shortcut key defined when the style was created.

❑ *Using a style does not limit the formatting you can apply to a text. It is still possible to modify the formatting of individual characters, words and/or paragraphs.*

To cancel the use of a style, open the **Style** list on the **Formatting** bar and choose the style called **Normal**, or press ⌘ ⇧ Shift *N*.

Modifying a style   ♦ **Format**
Style

♦ In the **Styles** list, select the one you wish to modify.

♦ Click the **Modify** button.

♦ Change the detail of the style.

♦ If you are in a document linked to the template, but not in the template itself, you can still change the style in the template by activating **Add to template**.

♦ Click **OK**.

♦ Modify other styles if you need to, then click **Close**.

Deleting a style

♦ **Format**
  Style

♦ In the **Styles** list, click the name of the style you wish to delete.

♦ Click the **Delete** button.

♦ Confirm by clicking **Yes**.

♦ Click **Close**.

❑ *Normal, Heading 1, Heading 2, Heading 3* are four styles created by Word in the NORMAL template: they cannot be deleted from your custom templates.

Automating the use of certain styles

Defining the style of the first text in a document

♦ Open the template concerned.

♦ At the beginning of the first paragraph of the template, apply the required style.

Defining the style that follows another style

♦ Open the template.

♦ **Format**
  Style

♦ Select the first style (the one which is to be followed).

♦ Click the **Modify** button.

♦ In the **Style for following paragraph** list box, click the name of the style which follows.

♦ If necessary, define or modify any other elements of the first style, then click **OK**.

Printing the list of styles

♦ Open the template, or a document containing the styles to print.

♦ **File**
Print...

♦ ☐ ⌘ P

♦ Open the **Print** list and choose **Styles**.

♦ Click **Print**.

The styles are printed in alphabetical order, along with their attributes.

Using styles from another template

♦ Apply to your document the styles already defined.

♦ **Format**
Style Gallery

On the left of the screen, there is a list of all existing templates. On the right, you can see the current document as it would appear if you used the styles of the selected template.

♦ Choose a **Template** in the list, and check the result in the **Preview of** box.

♦ When you are satisfied, click **OK** or, if no template is suitable, abandon using **Cancel**.

Using Autoformat for your document

This technique allows you to make use of Word's capacities to improve your presentation.

♦ Open the document.

♦ **Format
AutoFormat...**

♦ If necessary, click the **Options...** button.

♦ Personalise the AutoFormat options on the **AutoFormat** tab, then click **OK**.

♦ Choose **AutoFormat now** or **AutoFormat and review each change**, then click **OK**.

*If you choose **AutoFormat and review each change**, the Auto-Format dialog box appears:*

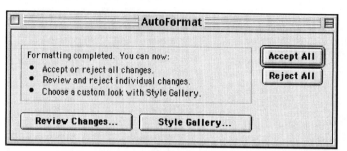

♦ You can choose to **Accept All** the new formatting, to **Reject All** and leave your document unchanged, or to **Review Changes** and check each modification one at a time.

If you choose this last option, Word stops at each of the revision marks placed in the text, and prompts you to accept or reject the change.

♦ If you have chosen the **Review Changes** option, click the **Find** button corresponding to the direction in which you wish to search.

Word stops at the first modification proposed. If you wish, you can reposition the dialog box, and scroll the text using the scroll cursor.

♦ Then choose:

Find   to go to the next mark.

Reject   to refuse the modification.

Undo   to reinstate a correction just cancelled.

When you reach the end of the document, Word proposes to review the beginning.

♦ At the end of the document, click **Cancel** in the dialog box displayed.

♦ Click **Cancel** again to close the dialog box.

♦ Click **Accept All** to return to the document.

. . . . *Personal notes* . . . .

**Creating
an AutoText entry**

*An AutoText entry allows you to use an abbreviation to insert a
text which you type repeatedly (address, form of words ...).*

Preparation before creation

♦ Does the text represented by the abbreviation (the future contents
of the AutoText) always have a specific format, or not ?

An AutoText is linked to the style in which it is created.

♦ Which abbreviation are you going to use (this will become the
name of the AutoText)?

*The name of an AutoText can be up to 31 characters long, inclu-
ding spaces. Short names, however, are more convenient. The
table below contains two examples of AutoTexts in preparation:
the text to insert, a description, formatting to apply to the text
and the name of the AutoText (the abbreviation used).*

First example	Mr. Andrew DELANEY 12 St Mark's Street MANCHESTER M12 5XJ		
	Address used in letters	style: ADDRESS blank lines below	DELANEY
Second example	Claire O'Brian Sales Manager		
	Signature used in letters	style: SIG	CLAIRE

Creating an AutoText

♦ If you want to make the AutoText available for use in any document, open a document linked to NORMAL or to the template on which you usually base your documents.

If the AutoText entry concerns a certain type of document created from a particular template, open a document based on that template.

♦ Activate the style associated with the AutoText.

♦ Enter the contents of the AutoText, not forgetting additional formatting and blank lines.

♦ Select the contents of the AutoText.

 ♦ **Insert**
AutoText
AutoText

♦ In the **Look in** list, choose the template where you want to create the AutoText.

♦ Give a name for the AutoText in the **Enter AutoText entries here** box.

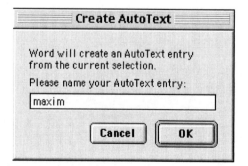

♦ Click **Add**.

 ♦ Click the **New** button on the **AutoText** toolbar.

♦ Enter a name for the AutoText.

♦ Click **OK**.

❏ *This technique creates the AutoText in the template which is selected under the **AutoText** tab of the **AutoCorrect** dialog box.*

Saving an AutoText list in a template

♦ If the AutoTexts have been created in a template other than NORMAL, you will be asked to save them when you close or save <u>the document</u>.

♦ If they have been created in NORMAL, you will be asked to save them as you leave the program.

Using an AutoText

First method

♦ Move the insertion point to the place where you want to insert.

♦ **Insert**
   AutoText
   AutoText

♦ If necessary, choose the template, which contains the AutoText, from the **Look in** list.

♦ Click the name of the AutoText.

♦ Click the **Insert** button.

Second method

♦ Position the insertion point where you want the contents of the AutoText to appear.

♦ Activate the style linked to the AutoText.

♦ **Insert**
   AutoText

At the bottom of the submenu, there is a list of the styles associated with AutoTexts in the current template.

♦ Select the style which contains the AutoText.

♦ Click the name of the AutoText to insert.

Third method

♦ Make sure that the **Show AutoComplete tip for AutoText and dates** check box is active in **Insert - AutoText - AutoText**.

♦ Place the insertion point where the contents of the AutoText should appear.

♦ Enter the name of the AutoText.

♦ When Word suggests the contents of the AutoText, press ⏎.

Printing the AutoTexts

♦ If the AutoTexts are stored in a template, a document based on that template should be active.

♦ **File**
   Print
♦ **P**

♦ In the **Print** pop-up menu, choose **AutoText entries**.

♦ Click **Print**.

❑ *First Word prints the AutoTexts belonging to the template, then those of NORMAL. They appear in alphabetical order.*

Managing existing AutoTexts

Deleting an AutoText

♦ **Insert**
   AutoText
   AutoText

♦ In the **Look in** list, select the template containing the AutoText.

♦ Click the name of the AutoText you wish to delete.

♦ Click the **Delete** button.

The name of the AutoText disappears immediately from the list.

♦ Close the dialog box.

Modifying the contents of an AutoText

♦ Type in and/or select the new contents.

♦ Create a new AutoText with the same name as the one you wish to modify.

♦ Confirm the modification by clicking **Yes** in the dialog box which appears.

♦ Enter.

❑ *When you modify or delete an AutoText, you modify the template. Remember to save it.*

. . . . *Personal notes* . . . .

Finding text   <u>By its contents</u>

♦ Position the insertion point where the search should begin.

♦ **Edit**   ♦ **F**
  Find

♦ Enter the text you need to find in the **Find what** box, deleting old search criteria if necessary.

*The **Find what** box takes up to 255 characters.*

♦ Click the **More** button, if necessary, to specify how you want the search carried out. Activate:

Match case   to find the text in question, written with the exact combination of upper and lower case letters entered in **Find what**.
For example, when searching for "lea"; if the option **Match case** is deactivated, Word will find "lea" of course, but also "Lea" and "LEA". To find only "lea", the option must be active.

Find whole words only   if the character string you are looking for constitutes a word.
For example, the text "late": if this option is deactivated, Word will find "late" but also "lateness", "relate" or "lateral"; if the option is active, only "late" will be found.

Use wildcards   to find text using more elaborate selection criteria (see Using wildcards below).

Sounds like   to find words sounding like the **Find what** text but spelled differently.

Find all word forms   respects word forms of the **Find what** text when replacing with the **Replace with** text.

♦ Use the **Search** pop-up menu to specify whether Word should search **Up** or **Down** from the position of the insertion point, or through **All** the document.

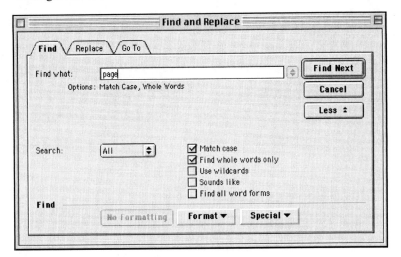

♦ Start the search with the **Find Next** button.

Almost immediately, the first occurrence of the text in the document is selected.

♦ If this first text is the one you are looking for, close the dialog box using **Cancel**; if it is not, continue by **Find Next**.

*Once the **Find and Replace** dialog box is closed, you can go on searching using* .

By its format

♦ Place the insertion point where you wish to start searching.

♦ **Edit**   ♦ ⌘ F
  Find

♦ Delete any text appearing in the **Find what** text box.

♦ Click the **Format** button.

♦ Choose the category of formatting which interests you from the options available.

♦ In the dialog box, activate the formats you are looking for and deactivate those you want Word to ignore. Click **OK**.

*Word returns to the first dialog box, so that you can specify additional criteria if you need to. The formats you have selected appear under **Format**.*

♦ Specify all the formats concerned by the search.

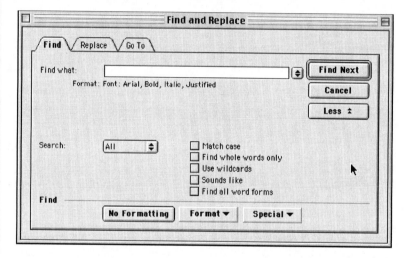

♦ Start the search by clicking the **Find Next** button.

♦ If the first text found is not the right one, click **Find Next** again. Close the dialog box once the text has been found.

*If you do not wish your format specification to be used for subsequent searches, click **No Formatting** to cancel the format before you close the dialog box.*

Rather than using the options associated with the **Format** button, you can use the **Formatting** toolbar or the keyboard.

**Replacing
one text
by another**

♦ Position the insertion point where you want Word to start looking for the text.

♦ **Edit
Replace**

♦ **H**

♦ Enter the text you need to find in the **Find what** box, deleting old search criteria if necessary.

♦ Go into the **Replace with** box, delete its existing contents and enter the new text.

♦ If necessary, click **More** and specify how you want the replacement to be carried out.

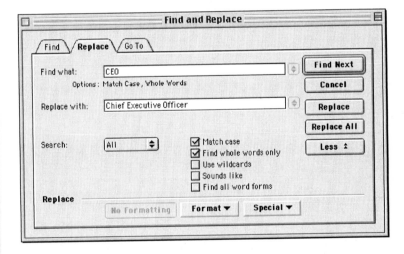

*The **Find whole words only** option is the same as the one in the
Find dialog box.*
*The **Match case** option has considerable importance here. If you
ask, for example, for BB to be replaced by Bluebird and the option is active, Word will find only occurrences of "BB" and will
replace them by "Bluebird". If the option is not active, Word will
find "BB" and replace it by "BLUEBIRD"; it will find "Bb" and
replace it by "Bluebird"; it will find "bb" and replace it by "bluebird".*

Word 98 for Macintosh

♦ If you want to check each text before it is replaced, click **Find Next** then **Replace**: to carry out all the replacements at once, click **Replace All**.

The number of replacements made is displayed in a window:

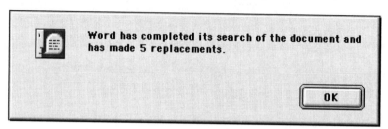

Word has completed its search of the document and has made 5 replacements.

OK

♦ Click **OK**.

♦ If necessary, shut the dialog box with the **Close** button.

Replacing a format by another

♦ Place the insertion point where Word is to start its search.

♦ **Edit**   ♦ ⌦ ⌘ **H**
   Replace

♦ If necessary, delete all old search and replacement criteria.

♦ Specify the existing format and the one to replace it.

♦ Chose to **Replace All**, or to carry out replacements one by one using the **Find Next** and **Replace** buttons.

♦ Click **OK** at the end of the procedure or close the dialog box by clicking **Close**.

Finding/replacing special characters

♦ **Edit**   ♦ ⌦ ⌘ **F** or ⌦ ⌘ **H**
   Find or **Replace**

♦ Proceed as for any other replacement (or search) but use the **Special** button to choose the symbol, punctuation mark... concerned.

120

The code representing the character appears.

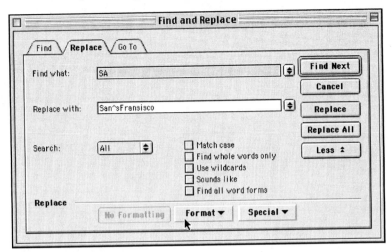

♦ Click **Replace All** or **Find Next**.

♦ When all the replacements are done, click **OK**, then **Close**.

Using wildcards

♦ **Edit**
Find or **Replace**

♦ ⌘ F or ⌘ H

♦ Give the text you want to find, using the following operators:

?	replaces one character.
*	replaces any string of characters.
[x-z]	replaces any character included in the range defined.
[]	replaces one of the characters specified between the brackets.
[!]	replaces any one character except those which appear between the brackets.
[!x-z]	replaces any one character except those in the range quoted between the brackets.

{n}   replaces exactly n occurrences of the preceding character or the preceding expression.

{n,m}   replaces from n to m occurrences of the preceding character or the preceding expression.

@   replaces one or several occurrences of the preceding character or the preceding expression.

<   replaces the beginning of a word.

>   replaces the end of a word.

Example	can be used to find	but will not find
?aw	saw - law - raw	thaw
s*w	saw - sinew - somehow	jigsaw
drive[i-r]	driver - driven	drives
fo[uw]l	foul - fowl	foal
th[!i]n	than - then	thin
[!n-r]ole	dole - hole - sole	pole - role
fil{2}	fill - fillet - filly	file - filial
can{1,2}	cane - canary - canny	
co@	cocoa - cocoon	
<(in)	into - ink - investigate	drive-in
(re)>	centre	rewrite

♦ Activate **Use wildcards**.

♦ Start the search.

Checking the grammar or spelling in a document

Setting off a check

♦ If the whole document is to be checked, position the insertion point at the top. If only a part of the text is concerned, select it.

When there is no selection, Word checks the entire document including margin notes, headers, footers...

♦ **Tools** ♦
Spelling and Grammar

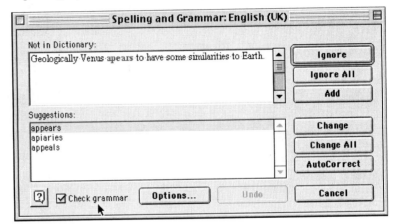

Word starts to read the document, then stops at the first word it does not recognise.
Words are queried for three main reasons: the word is unknown (does not occur in the application's dictionary), the word is repeated (example: I know that that is true), the word is entered with an unusual combination of upper and lower case letters (example: LEtter).

❑ Spelling is checked against Word's main dictionary and as many custom dictionaries as you like (by default, there exists only one: Custom Dictionary).

♦ If you prefer Word to check spelling only, deactivate **Check grammar**.

Customising the spelling check

♦ Go into the **Spelling and Grammar** dialog box and click the **Options** button.

♦ Choose whether or not to **Ignore words in UPPERCASE** and/or **Ignore words with numbers**.

These options are useful if, for example, the document contains a list of proper nouns.

♦ Choose whether or not to activate **Always suggest corrections**. If this option is deactivated, Word does not provide a **Suggestions** list.

Using a custom dictionary

♦ Click the **Options...** button in the **Spelling and Grammar** dialog box.

♦ To use an existing dictionary, click its name in the **Custom dictionaries** list.
To <u>add</u> a new custom dictionary, click the **Dictionaries** button then the **New** button, give a name for the new dictionary then click **Save**.

The new dictionary appears in the list of existing dictionaries. It is automatically open (this is indicated by the check mark preceding its name).

♦ To close an open dictionary, click the check box by its name.

The check mark disappears: it is closed.

♦ To open a dictionary, click the same check box.

♦ Click **OK** to close the **Custom Dictionaries** dialog box.

♦ Click **OK** to close the page of options.

Managing correctly spelt words

♦ Click:

Ignore	to leave the word as it is and continue the spelling check.
Ignore All	to ignore the word each time it occurs during the check.

♦ To add the word to a custom dictionary so that Word will recognise it the next time, click the **Add** button.

Correcting badly spelt words

♦ If the correct version of the word is proposed in the **Suggestions** list, double-click the right spelling (or click once then click **Change**).

If you know the correct spelling, enter it in the text box and click **Change**.

> If you enter by clicking the **Change All** button, then the same error is automatically corrected if it recurs in the document.

Deleting repetitions

♦ Click the **Delete** button.

Managing errors in grammar

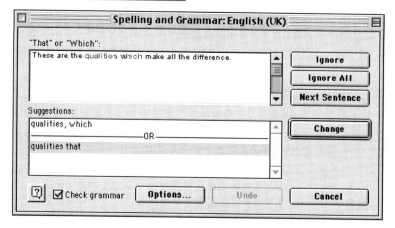

♦ To correct a grammar mistake, correct the text in the text box, then click **Change**.

♦ If you do not wish to correct the text, click:

Ignore or   To leave the text unchanged and continue the
Ignore All   check.

Next Sentence	To move the check on to the next sentence, even though the current one may contain further errors.

♦ At the end of the check, click **OK**.

> *The last correction carried out can be undone by the **Undo** option in the **Spelling and Grammar** dialog box.*

Consulting a custom dictionary

♦ Find out where the dictionary is stored: go into the **Tools - Preferences** dialog box and onto the **Spelling and Grammar** tab, click the **Dictionaries** button then the dictionary which interests you: make a note of its path.

♦ Use **File - Open** and continue as for any other file.

Activating AutoCorrect

*If the **AutoCorrect** options are active, Word corrects common mistakes as you type (for instance, if you type "teh" Word will replace it with "the").*

♦ **Tools**
  AutoCorrect

♦ Activate or deactivate the first three options.

♦ If there is a spelling or typing error you tend to repeat, type the incorrect version of the word in the **Replace** box, and the correct version in the **With** box.

AutoCorrect

AutoCorrect / AutoFormat As You Type / AutoText / AutoFormat

☑ Correct TWo INitial CApitals

☑ Capitalize first letter of sentences

☑ Capitalize names of days

☑ Replace text as you type

Replace: With: ⊙ Plain text   ○ Formatted text

| trafic | traffic |

traditionalyl	traditionally
transfered	transferred
truely	truly
truley	truly
tryed	tried
tthe	the
tyhat	that

Exceptions...

Add   Delete

Cancel   OK

♦ Click the **Add** button.

♦ Repeat for any more habitual mistakes you can think of.

♦ End by **OK**.

Specifying the language used

♦ **Tools**
Language
Set Language...

♦ Double-click the language used in the **Mark selected text as** list.

❑ *The spelling, grammar, hyphens..., are checked according to the language chosen.*

> *If all new documents are to be written in a particular language, click the language, click **Default** and confirm.*

**Counting
the sentences/
words
in a document**

♦ If only part of the document is concerned, select it.

♦ **Tools
Word Count**

♦ Consult the resulting statistics, then click **Close**.

. . . . *Personal notes* . . . .

Using the thesaurus

<u>Displaying the thesaurus</u>

♦ Place the insertion point in the word, or just after it.

♦ **Tools**
  Language
  Thesaurus...

♦ ⎡⇧ Shift⎤ ⎡F 7⎤

*In the **Meanings** list on the left, the different meanings of the word are listed. On the right all the synonyms of the selected meaning of the word appear.*

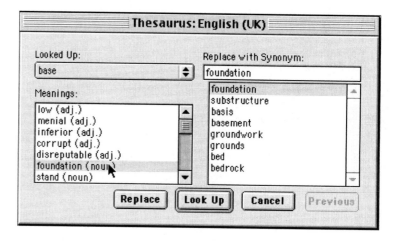

<u>Finding the right synonym</u>

♦ In the **Meanings** list, click the appropriate meaning.

♦ To list synonyms of one of the synonyms, double-click it.

♦ Click **Previous** to return to the previous word looked up.

<u>Leaving the thesaurus</u>

♦ If you wish to replace the word selected in the text with one of its synonyms, click the one in question, then click the **Replace** button; if you prefer to leave the original word, click **Cancel**.

Hyphenating Words

Breaking words up and hyphenating them smoothes irregularities along the margin, or, in justified alignment, reduces the space left between each word.

♦ To carry out hyphenation of the whole document, place the insertion point at the beginning, otherwise select the passage concerned.

♦ **Tools**
Language
Hyphenation

♦ Determine how hyphenation is to be carried out:

Automatically hyphenate document	Word does the hyphenating without asking for confirmation from you. The choice becomes active when you click **OK**; words are broken up automatically as you type.
Hyphenate words in CAPS	If this choice is deactivated, Word will not hyphenate words with capital letters.
Hyphenation zone	If the space available on a line is superior to the value of this zone, Word tries to break up the first word of the following line. Unless you modify it, the value proposed is 0.63 cm.
Limit consecutive hyphens to	Indicate here the maximum number of consecutive lines that can end in hyphens. The usual value is three.
Manual	Word asks for confirmation before hyphenating a word.

*When you activate the **Manual** choice, a flashing cursor appears at the proposed hyphenation: if you accept, the hyphen and its preceding text will go up to the line above. The dotted bar represents the end of the line. Other hyphens which may appear correspond to other possibilities for hyphenating the word:*

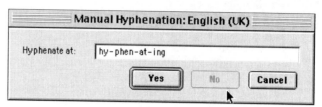

You can move the hyphen using the ☐→ or ☐← key, but if you go beyond the limit of space in the line, Word memorises your instruction, but cannot follow it.

♦ Decide whether the hyphenation is acceptable (**Yes** or **No** buttons), or whether the hyphen should be moved (☐→ or ☐← then the **Yes** button).

♦ Click **OK**.

♦ Place the insertion point where you wish to hyphenate.

♦ Insert an optional hyphen by pressing ☐ ⌘ - .

❑ *It is important to use this optional hyphen for manual hyphenation: if, after modification of the paragraph, the word in question is no longer at the end of a line, the hyphen will not be printed.*

❑ *When the special characters are visible, optional hyphens have their own particular symbol.*

Using master documents

A master document groups together several sub-documents for the purposes of numbering their pages, adding headings, notes...

♦ Create a new document using the template common to all the sub-documents.

♦ **View**
Master Document

♦ Insert each sub-document by clicking [⬛].

The content of each sub-document appears.

♦ Save the master document.

♦ If necessary, number the pages, headings... from within the master document.

♦ To print all the sub-documents, print the master document.

Creating a summary of a document

♦ Open the document concerned.

♦ **Tools**
AutoSummarize...

Word takes a few seconds to produce the summary dialog box.

♦ Choose the **Type of summary** you require.

AutoSummarize

Word has examined the document and picked the sentences most relevant to the main theme.

Type of summary

Highlight key points

Insert an executive summary or abstract at the top of the document

Create a new document and put the summary there

Hide everything but the summary without leaving the original document

Length of summary

Percent of original: 25%

Summary: 806 words in 44 sentences
Original document: 3,183 words in 146 sentences

☑ Update document statistics (click Properties on the File menu)

Cancel   OK

♦ Click **OK**.

. . . . *Personal notes* . . . .

Creating notes

Footnotes and/or endnotes can be added to expand on the contents of a document.

♦ Position the insertion point at the place in the document where you want to insert a note reference.

♦ **Insert**
 Footnote

♦ Specify whether you are creating a **Footnote** or an **Endnote**.

♦ Choose between:

AutoNumber   to leave the numbering of notes to Word.

Custom mark   to create your own mark referring to a note.

Custom marks can contain no more than 10 characters.

♦ Click **OK**.

*In **Normal** view, a box for entering the text of the note appears at the bottom of the window. This is the note pane.*

♦ Enter the text of the note.

The style reserved for the text of a note is called "Footnote text", the one for the marks referring to a note is called "Footnote reference".

♦ Click inside the document or press F6 .

Word keeps a place at the bottom of the page so that the text of a footnote is printed on the same page as the note reference.

The first note of a page is separated from the text by a horizontal line.

♦ To see the contents of a note, point to the note reference (without clicking) or use the note pane.

*When you point to the note reference, the contents of the note appears in a ScreenTip, providing the corresponding option is active under the **View** tab of the **Tools - Preferences** dialog box.*

Using the note pane

Using the notes to move around the text

♦ Go into the note pane.

♦ Move from note to note within the pane.

Notice that the document in the workspace is scrolled up or down to correspond to the note you are looking at.

Closing/opening the pane

♦ **View**

Deactivate or activate the **Footnotes** option.

*When the pane is open, you can shut it by clicking the **Close** button.*
When it is closed, it can be opened by a double-click on a note reference.

Managing existing notes

To manage notes, work with the note references, and not with the text in the pane.

♦ To modify the content of a note, double-click the reference of the note, then carry out your modifications.

♦ To delete a note, select its note reference then press the Del key.

♦ To move a note, move the note reference as you would a text.

❏ *The notes are automatically renumbered.*

Modifying the general presentation of notes

Modifying styles

♦ Modify the styles: **Footnote Reference**, **Endnote Reference**, **Footnote Text**, **Endnote Text** so that the notes look as you want them to.

Modifying the position of a note

♦ **Insert**
   Footnote

♦ Click the **Options...** button then activate the appropriate tab.

♦ Use the **Place at** pop-up menu to indicate the note's position on the printed page:

	Place at	Position on Page
For footnotes	**Bottom of page**	in the bottom margin
	Beneath text	in the lower part of the page
For endnotes	**End of section**	at the end of a section
	End of document	at the end of the document

♦ Click **OK**.

♦ Leave the dialog box by **Close**, or by **OK** if you have added a new note.

Modifying the numbering

♦ **Insert**
  Footnote

♦ Click the **Options** button.

♦ Use the **Number format** pop-up menu to change the way the numbers look.

♦ To change the first number, enter the new one in the **Start at** box.

This is mainly to correct the numbering when you break up a long document into several smaller ones.

♦ Specify whether numbering is to be continuous throughout the document, by activating the **Continuous** option of the **Numbering** group, or whether it should **Restart each section**, or even **Restart each page**.

```
┌─────────────────────────────────────────────────┐
│ ══════════════ Note Options ══════════════       │
│                                                   │
│  ╱ All Footnotes ╲╱ All Endnotes ╲               │
│  ┌──────────────────────────────────────┐        │
│  │                                        │        │
│  │  Place at:        │Bottom of page  │▲▼││        │
│  │                                        │        │
│  │  Number format:   │A, B, C, ...    │  ▲▼││      │
│  │                                        │        │
│  │  Start at:        │A               │  ▲▼││      │
│  │                                        │        │
│  │  Numbering:       ● Continuous        │        │
│  │                   ○ Restart each section│       │
│  │                   ○ Restart each page  │        │
│  └──────────────────────────────────────┘        │
│                                                   │
│  ┌──────────┐        ┌────────┐ ┌──────────┐     │
│  │ Convert… │        │ Cancel │ │    OK    │     │
│  └──────────┘        └────────┘ └──────────┘     │
└─────────────────────────────────────────────────┘
```

♦ Click **OK**.

♦ Leave by **Close**, or by **OK** if you have made changes.

Working with bookmarks

A bookmark allows you to mark a place in a text, so that you can find it immediately.

Creating a bookmark

♦ If going to a bookmark involves selecting a passage of text, select that text. If going to a bookmark is simply a matter of moving the insertion point, put the insertion point in the position required.

♦ **Insert Bookmark...**

♦

♦ Enter the name of the new bookmark.

The name of a bookmark can be up to 20 characters long. It must start with a letter and must not contain any spaces.

♦ Click the **Add** button.

Deleting a bookmark

♦ **Insert**
  Bookmark...

♦ ⌃ ⌘ ⇧ Shift F5

♦ In the **Bookmark name** list, select the bookmark to delete.

♦ Click the **Delete** button.

♦ Click the **Close** button.

Using a bookmark

♦ **Insert**
Bookmark...

♦

♦ Under **Sort by**, choose to sort the bookmark list by the **Location** of the bookmark in the document, or by its **Name**.

♦ Double-click the bookmark you want to reach.

♦ Shut the dialog box using the **Close** button.

> *Bookmarks can also be reached via **Edit - Go To**.*

. . . . *Personal notes* . . . .

Constructing the outline of a document

Making an outline not only allows you to put together a table of contents, but also facilitates moving around in the document. There are two ways of making an outline:

– using Outline view
– assigning importance levels to each type of paragraph.

Using Outline view

Activating/leaving Outline view

♦ **View**
  Outline

The Outline toolbar replaces the ruler, and each paragraph is preceded by a white square.

♦ Leave outline view by **View - Normal, View - Outline Layout** or **View - Page Layout**.

Entering a heading into the outline

♦ Place the insertion point in the heading paragraph.

♦ Apply one of the following styles, depending on the importance of the heading:

Heading 1	main headings
Heading 2	subheadings
Heading 3	sub-subheadings.

Applying the styles Heading 1, Heading 2, Heading 3... obviously cancels any existing formatting of your own. You can however, customise these styles once they are in place. A cross to the left of the text marks it out as being a heading in an outline.

❑ *If a normal paragraph has been defined as a heading by mistake, return to it and click* .

To change the presentation of headings, modify the corresponding styles: *Heading 1, Heading 2, Heading 3.*

**Assigning
an importance
level to
a paragraph**

This technique allows you to create an outline without losing the existing formatting.

♦ Select the paragraph which corresponds to the heading.

♦ **Format
Paragraph**

♦ In the **Outline level** list, choose the level for the heading (a level between 1 and 9).

♦ Click **OK**.

♦ Repeat for each level of heading.

If you plan to number the headings in an outline created using this technique, put the corresponding paragraphs into a style which includes numbering.
You can also include an outline level in a style.

Using outlines

Determining what appears in Outline view

♦ Go into **Outline** view.

♦ Display and hide the various levels of text as follows:

	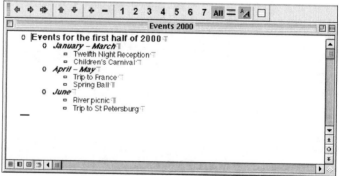	
to display headings of a corresponding level and above	buttons **1** to **7**	Ctrl ⇧ Shift and the digit (chosen from the line of digits on the alphanumeric section of the keyboard)
to view the whole document	**All** button	
to hide the text under the heading	double-click the cross preceding the heading or click **−**	
to display the text under the heading	click **+**	
to promote a heading	click **⇐**	
to demote a heading	click **⇒**	

```
⇐ ⇒ ⇔   ⇑ ⇓   ⇕ −   1 2 3 4 5 6 7 All ＝ ᴬA □

                    Events 2000

   o  Events for the first half of 2000 ¶
      o  January – March ¶
         □  Twelfth Night Reception ¶
         □  Children's Carnival ¶
      o  April – May ¶
         □  Trip to France ¶
         □  Spring Ball ¶
      o  June ¶
         □  River picnic ¶
         □  Trip to St Petersburg ¶
   —
```

Example of a collapsed outline

Changing the order of headings

♦ Go into **Outline** view.

♦ Drag the heading by the cross in front of it.

The heading, any associated subheadings, and the text are moved simultaneously.

Using the outline to move around the document

♦ Go into **Outline** view.

♦ Click the heading you want to reach in the document.

♦ Leave **Outline** view.

❏ *You could also use the Document Map.*

> *To print just an outline of the document, choose the headings you want printed, and print.*

Numbering headings in an outline

♦ Position the insertion point on the first heading of the list that you want to number (any view can be active).

♦ **Format**
   Bullets and Numbering...
   Outline Numbered tab

Numbering headings created using Heading styles

♦ Choose one of the options where the word "Heading" appears.

♦ To customise the numbering, click **Customize.**

♦ Customise the numbering to suit you.

♦ Click **OK**.

❏ *To delete the numbering from an outline, display the titles concerned in Outline view, go into **Format - Bullets and Numbering**
and click the **None** frame.*

Numbering headings which have custom styles

◆ Under the **Outline Numbered** tab, choose the option which comes closest to what you require.

◆ Click **Customize**, and then **More**, if necessary.

◆ In the **Link level to style** list, choose the appropriate style.

◆ Define the level for each style.

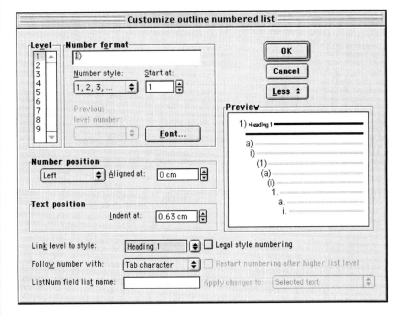

◆ Click **OK**.

Constructing a table of contents from an outline

◆ Place the insertion point where the table is to be inserted.

◆ **Insert
Index and Tables...**

◆ Activate the **Table of Contents** tab.

◆ In the **Formats** list, choose the one you prefer. You can check the result in the **Preview** frame.

♦ Indicate which elements are to be included in the table, and how this is to be done: should the table **Show page numbers**? If so, do you wish to **Right align page numbers**? Up to what level should Word **Show levels** of headings?

♦ Finally, for all formats apart from **Simple** and **Modern**, you can modify the **Tab leader** character.

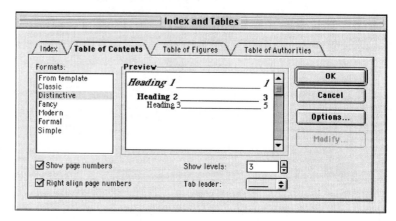

♦ Click **OK**.

❑ *A table created by this method uses the styles **TOC1** and **TOC2**, which you can, of course, modify (spacing before and after, tab stops, font ...).*

❑ *Be sure that your page numbers will not be modified again, before inserting your table of contents.*

Inserting a table of figures

♦ Place the insertion point where the table of figures is to be inserted.

♦ **Insert**
  Index and Tables...

♦ Activate the **Table of Figures** tab.

♦ In the **Caption Label** box, indicate whether the items in the table are figures, equations, photos...

♦ Chose from the **Formats** list. Check the result in the **Preview** frame.

♦ Activate the **Include label and number** check box, if appropriate.

♦ Click **OK**.

Making an index   *Here is an example of the type of index you might draw up:*

```
S
Sites of Geographical Interest
        Death Valley..............................4; 10
        Great Valley..................................5
        Mount Whitney.....................4; 5; 10
        National Parks
                Redwood National Park.........4
                Yosemite Park..................5
```

Defining an entry for the index

♦ If the entry you want in the index is already entered, select it, otherwise place the insertion point where the subject to be indexed is discussed.

♦ **Insert**
Index and Tables...
Index tab
Mark Entry button

♦ If appropriate, specify the **Main entry** in the box provided.

♦ If necessary go to the **Subentry** box and type in the secondary entry.

♦ If you wish to create further entry levels, type a colon (:) before entering the text.

◆ Format the text using shortcut keys.

◆ Enter by the **Mark** button.

*The **Cancel** button is replaced by a **Close** button.*

If the nonprinting characters are visible, you will be able to see the inserted field {XE. ...}.

◆ Click **Close.**

Inserting the index

◆ Place the insertion point where you want to put the index.

◆ **Insert
Index and Tables...**

◆ Activate the **Index** tab, if necessary.

♦ Choose a look for the subentries under **Type:**

Indented   The subentries are indented in relation to the main entries, and they are one underneath the other.

Run-in   The entries are listed one underneath the other, but the subentries are listed side by side, separated by semicolons.

♦ Indicate the **Format** you want and check its appearance in the **Preview** frame.

♦ If you wish, and when it is possible, specify the number of **Columns** and the **Tab leader** character; indicate whether or not you want to **Right align page numbers** and use separate **Headings for accented letters**.

♦ Click **OK**.

❏ The styles used in the table are called *Index 1*, *Index 2*... They can, of course, be modified.

❏ As with the table of contents, check that the document's page numbers are correct and permanent before inserting the index.

. . . . *Personal notes* . . . .

Inserting a table

There are several ways of doing this.

♦ Position the insertion point where you want to insert the table.

♦ **Table**
 Insert Table...

♦ Specify the **Number of columns** and the **Number of rows**.

The columns in Word tables correspond to columns of text (or numbers, drawings ...) and the rows to rows of cells and not to lines of text.

♦ Let Word decide the width of each column by choosing **Auto** in the **Column width** box, or enter your own value.

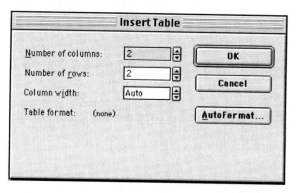

*The choice **Auto** makes the columns as wide as possible given their number and the space available.*

♦ Click **OK**.

❑ A table can contain a maximum of 63 columns.

A table can also be inserted using the ▦ button.

♦ If necessary, display the **Tables and Borders** toolbar.

♦ Check that the  tool is active (click it to activate it).

The mouse pointer takes the shape of a pencil.

♦ Choose a style, thickness and colour for the outline of the table.

♦ Drag to draw the outline.

♦ If you wish, choose a different style, thickness and/or colour for your lines, then draw in rows and columns.

♦ Click  again.

❑ *The advantage of this technique is that you can decide the height of the rows, the width of the columns, and the type of lines used.*

Moving around a table

♦ With the mouse, use the normal pointing and clicking techniques.

♦ With the keyboard, use the following keys:

⇥ / ⇧ Shift ⇥	the cell to the right/left
↓ / ↑	the cell below/above
⌥ ↖ / ⌥ ↘	the first/last cell of the active row
⌥ Pg Up / ⌥ Pg Dn	the first/last cell of the active column.

Selecting in a table

♦ Depending on what you are selecting, use one of the following techniques:

To select a CELL		
Position the mouse pointer inside the cell at the left (it adopts the form of an arrow pointing top right) and click		→‖ or ⇧ Shift →‖
To select a COLUMN		
Position the mouse pointer above the column (it adopts the form of a black arrow pointing down) and click	activate a cell from the column then **Table** **Select column**	
To select a ROW		
Position the mouse pointer at the left of the row (it adopts the form of an arrow pointing top right) and click	activate a cell from the row then **Table** **Select Row**	
To select the TABLE		
Hold down the ⇧ Shift button while clicking, or drag over the table	click inside the table **Table** **Select table**	⌃ ⌘ ⇥ T

♦ To cancel the selection, click outside it.

Filling in a table

♦ Activate the cell where you want to start writing.

♦ Enter the contents of the cell as you would for any paragraph. Word takes care of line breaks.

> *Cells are formatted in the same way as paragraphs.*

Placing and using tabs in a table

♦ Position your tab stops as usual.

♦ For any tab other than a decimal one, press [Ctrl][→]; in the case of a decimal tab, the value you enter is automatically aligned with the tab stop.

Inserting a column

♦ Place the insertion point in the column to the left of the position where you are going to insert the new one. To insert a new column at the end of a table, click just after the line to the right of the last column.

♦ Select the column containing the insertion point, even if it is the non-existent one after the last column of the table.

♦ **Table**
  Insert Columns

  The new column is added. It has the characteristics of the one you selected, or of the column which used to be the last one.

Inserting a row

Before an existing row

♦ Select the row just under the position where you are going to insert the new one.

♦ **Table**
  Insert Rows

  The new row adopts the characteristics of the one you selected.

At the bottom of the table

♦ Click inside the last cell of the table and press [→].

Inserting cells

♦ Select the cells which come after the position where you are going to insert the new ones.

♦ **Table**
Insert Cells...

Word proposes two different ways of moving the selected cells to make room for the insertion. You also have the option of inserting a row or a column.

♦ Decide what to do with the selected cells:

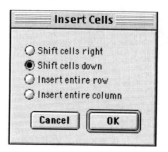

♦ Click **OK**.

Deleting rows/ columns/cells

Rows and/or columns

♦ Select the rows/columns you want deleted.

♦ **Table**
Delete Rows or **Delete Columns**

Cells

♦ Select the cells to be deleted.

♦ **Table**
Delete Cells...

♦ Decide what should happen to the remaining cells:

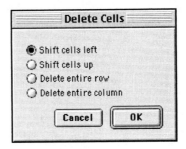

You can also choose to delete the whole row or column.

♦ Click **OK**.

Splitting a table in two

♦ Place the insertion point in the row below the point where you are going to split the table.

♦ **Table**
Split Table

♦

Your table splits into two tables separated by a paragraph.

Merging cells

It is possible to transform several cells into a single cell. In the table below, four cells have been merged to obtain the one containing the word "APRIL".

four cells have merged to create this one

	APRIL			
Personnel Concerned	04	11	18	25
MEECH A.	■			
BARRY M.				
GARNER P.		■		
FLOYD Y.				

♦ Display the **Tables and Borders** toolbar (**View - Toolbars - Tables and Borders**).

♦ Select the cells you wish to merge.

♦ **Table**
   Merge Cells

♦ Click the button.

The mouse pointer takes the shape of an eraser.

♦ Drag to erase the line which separates the cells you wish to merge.

♦ Click ✎ again to deactivate it.

Splitting cells   *This is the opposite of merging: one cell is split into two or more.*

♦ Select the cell(s) you wish to split.

♦ **Table**
   Split Cells ⊞

♦ If Word should first merge all the selected cells into one and then divide the resulting cell into rows and columns, activate **Merge cells before split**.
If the option is not active, each cell in the selection will be divided into rows and/or columns.

♦ Give the **Number of columns** and/or the **Number of rows** you wish to create.

♦ Click **OK**.

**Sorting
a table**

♦ Click inside the table which needs sorting.

♦ **Table
Sort**

Note that you can sort by up to three different criteria.

♦ For each of these:

– select the name or number of the column in the **Sort by** box,

– indicate what **Type** of data the column contains,

– choose whether the data should be sorted in **Ascending** or **Descending** order.

♦ In the **My list has** frame, click **Header row** to exclude the first row from sorting, or **No header row** if it is to be sorted like any other.

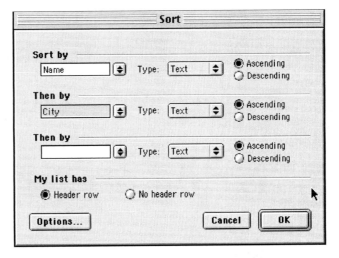

♦ When all the criteria have been defined, click **OK**.

If you are not satisfied with the new order of the data, use the [⤺ ▼] *button to restore the original order.*

Sorting one column of a table

♦ Select the column to be sorted.

♦ **Table**
Sort

♦ Check that the name/number of the column appears in the first **Sort by** box.

♦ Click the **Options** button.

♦ Activate **Sort column only** in the **Sort options** box.

♦ Click **OK** twice.

Converting text into a table

You can transform columns of text separated by tabs into a table.

♦ Select the text.

♦ **Table**
Convert Text To Table

♦ Confirm by **OK**.

❏ *A new column is produced at each tab character. A new row is produced at each end of paragraph or line break character.*

Managing ranges of cells in a table

♦ To copy cells or to move them elsewhere, proceed as for text, using the **Copy, Cut** and **Paste** commands from the **Edit** menu (or the corresponding buttons and shortcut keys).

Fixing column headings

If the table takes up several pages, this technique allows the column headings to be printed at the top of each page.

♦ Select the rows containing the headings.

♦ **Table**
Headings

Modifying column width/row height

One column/row

♦ Point to the line <u>at the right</u> of the column you wish to modify, or point to the marker representing the row on the ruler.

When the mouse pointer is correctly positioned it takes the form ⊣╟⊢ .

♦ Drag to increase or decrease the size of the column/row. Depending on how you drag, you obtain different results:

mouse alone	to modify the width of the particular column and compensate by changing the width of the column on the right.
with ⇧Shift	to modify the width of the particular column without adjusting any others. The overall width of the table is affected.
with ⌘ ⇧Shift	to modify the width of the particular column and adjust all the columns to the right, to preserve the overall width of the table.

♦ To modify the height of row, drag the horizontal line beneath the row.

While you are dragging, the mouse pointer looks like this: ⊥⊤

❑ *If you hold down the* ⌥ *key as you drag, the dimensions of the column/row appear on the ruler.*

Several columns/rows

♦ Select the columns, or rows: they will all be given the same new width/height.

♦ **Table** ~~Table Properties~~
Cell Height and Width...

♦ Activate the **Column** or **Row** tab.

Word displays the columns or rows to be modified.

♦ Enter the new width of the columns (**Width of columns...**).

To adapt the width of the columns to their contents, click the ***AutoFit*** *button.*

or
In the **Height of Rows** list, choose between:

Auto   to let Word decide the height.

At least   to define a minimum height.

Exactly   to define a fixed height.

♦ If you have activated **At least** or **Exactly**, enter the height in the **At** box.

♦ If the **Next Column/Previous Column** or the **Next Row/Previous Row** also needs modifying click the appropriate button to continue the process. When you have finished, click the **OK** button.

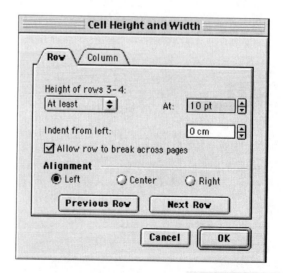

Standardising widths/heights

♦ Select the rows or columns to which you want to give the same height/width.

♦ **Table**
  Distribute Rows Evenly or **Distribute Columns Evenly**

Standardising the height/width of selected rows/columns does not effect the overall size of the table.

**Formatting
a table
automatically**

♦ Click inside the table you wish to format.

♦ **Table**
  Table AutoFormat...

♦ In the **Formats** list, choose the look closest to what you have in mind: check by looking in **Preview**.

♦ If you wish, choose from the **Formats to apply**, and indicate what they should apply to (under **Apply special formats to**).

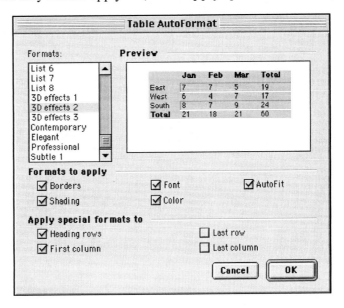

♦ Click **OK**.

Modifying lines in a table

♦ Select the cells concerned, or the whole table.

♦ If necessary, display the **Tables and Borders** toolbar.

♦ Add borders as you require.

Positioning a table on the page

♦ Click inside the table.

♦ **Table**
Cell Height and Width...

♦ If necessary, activate the **Row** tab.

♦ In the **Alignment** group, choose the position you want for the table.

❏ The ***Indent from left*** *option in this dialog box enables you to indent selected rows from the left margin by the number of centimetres you indicate in the box provided.*

. . . . *Personal notes* . . . .

Adding up a column/row

♦ If necessary, display the **Tables and Borders** toolbar.

♦ Click the cell where you want to display the result.

♦ Click $\boxed{\Sigma}$.

By default, Word adds the cells above the result cell.

Managing a table as with a spreadsheet

Basic principles

♦ Each column is identified by a letter (the first column is A, the second column is B ...) and each row by a number (the first row is 1, the second row is 2 ...). The cell reference is the association of its column letter with its row number (A2, B5...).

♦ To refer to consecutive cells, give the reference of the first cell, type a colon (:), and the reference of the last cell (eg. C2:C4).
To refer to non-consecutive cells, use the comma as the separator (eg. B5,D5).

Entering a calculation formula

♦ Activate the result cell.

♦ **Table**
Formula

♦ In the **Formula** box, enter your formula after the = sign, using the cell references and the following mathematical operators:

-	subtraction
/	division
*	multiplication
%	percentage calculation
^	to the power of ...
+	addition

Using an integrated function on a range of cells

♦ Delete any text from the **Formula** box, but leave the = sign.

♦ Choose the appropriate function from the **Paste function** list.

♦ In the **Formula** box, between brackets, indicate the range of cells involved in the calculation:

Above	for all cells above the one selected
Below	for all cells below
Left	for those to the left
Right	for those to the right
cell ref:cell ref	for consecutive cells
cell ref,cell ref	for non-consecutive cells.

Formatting the result of a calculation

♦ Choose from the **Number format** list.
Examples of the effect of different formats on the number -3637.54:

# ##0	-3 638
# ##0.00	-3 637.54
£# ##0.00;(£# ##0.00)	(£3 637.54)
0	-3638
0%	-3638%
0.00	-3637.54
0.00%	-3637.54%

```
┌─────────────────────────────────────────────┐
│                  Formula                      │
├─────────────────────────────────────────────┤
│  Formula:                                     │
│  ┌─────────────────────────────────────────┐ │
│  │ =AVERAGE(A2,D2)                         │ │
│  └─────────────────────────────────────────┘ │
│  Number format:                               │
│  ┌───────────────────────────────────────┐┌─┐│
│  │ £#,##0.00;(£#,##0.00)                  ││⬍││
│  └───────────────────────────────────────┘└─┘│
│  Paste function:        Paste bookmark:       │
│  ┌─────────────────┐┌─┐ ┌─────────────────┐┌┐│
│  │                 ││⬍│ │                 ││⬍││
│  └─────────────────┘└─┘ └─────────────────┘└┘│
│                    ┌──────────┐ ┌──────────┐  │
│                    │  Cancel  │ │    OK    │  │
│                    └──────────┘ └──────────┘  │
└─────────────────────────────────────────────┘
```

♦ Click **OK** to insert the formula.

❏ *Every calculation result is in fact the result of a **FIELD**.*

❏ *The values appear if you are viewing results, and not if you are viewing field codes.*

Displaying/hiding field codes

♦ To display or hide the field codes for a whole document, press ⌥ F9 .
To display or hide a particular field code, place the insertion point in the field and press ⇧ Shift F9 .

Towns	01/04	02/04	03/04	Total
Oxford	584 000	598 000	630 000	{ =sum(left) }
Dudley	960 000	953 000	940 000	{ =sum(left) }
Stoke	576 000	553 000	573 000	{ =sum(left) }
Total Midlands	{ =sum(above) }	{ =sum(above) }	{ =sum(above) }	{ =sum(above) }
Average Midlands	{ =average(b2:b4) }	{ =average(c2:c4) }	{ =average(d2:d4) }	{ =average(e2:e4) }

The formulas entered appear between braces. It is the formulas, not the results, that are the real contents of the fields, so that if one of the values in the calculation changes, the result is automatically adjusted.

CALCULATIONS

Updating a field

♦ Place the insertion point in the field concerned.

♦ Press F9 .

To update a field, you can hold down Ctrl as you click in the field, then click **Update Field**.

. . . . *Personal notes* . . . .

**Using
the Microsoft
Graph
Application**

*This application enables you to present data in the form of a chart
(graph).*

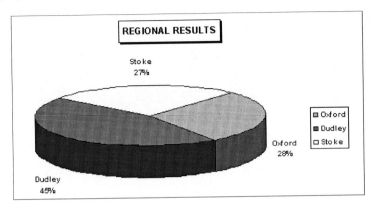

Starting the application

♦ If the data you are going to represent are already entered in a
document, copy them into the clipboard.

♦ Place the insertion point where you want to put the chart.

♦ **Insert
   Object...**
   double-click **Microsoft Graph 98 Chart**

Two objects appear on the screen: a **Chart** surrounded by a hatched border, and a **Datasheet** window containing the data represented in the chart. This is not your data: it is given as an example.

♦ It is a good idea to move the **Datasheet** window so that the chart is visible too.

If you are familiar with the spreadsheet Excel, you will recognise this presentation.

Clearing the contents of cells

♦ Select the cells to be cleared.

From one application to another, the techniques for selecting with the mouse remain the same.

♦ **Edit**
Clear...

*It is possible to clear the **Contents** of the cells, their **Format**, or both (**All**).*

♦ Choose what you want cleared.

❏*Notice that the chart reacts to these modifications step by step.*

Entering data

♦ Click in the first cell.

♦ Enter the data to be represented, or insert the contents of the clipboard.

Enter the text as you would in any Word table or transfer data from the clipboard as you would in any application.

Selecting an object in a chart

♦ Click the object.

Each object selected is surrounded by handles. Black handles indicate that the object can be resized or moved elsewhere.

The surest way to select the axes is to click one of the tick mark labels along one of the axes.

Modifying column width

♦ Select a cell in each column concerned.

♦ **Format**
Column Width...

♦ Enter the new width in the **Column width** box.

♦ Click **OK**.

Deleting a row/column

♦ Select each row/column to be deleted by clicking its label.

♦ **Edit**
  Delete

Specifying whether the data are in rows or columns

♦ **Data**
  Series in Rows or **Series in Columns**

Changing the type of chart

♦ **Chart**
  Chart Type

A list of all the main chart types appears.

♦ Choose a type from the **Chart type** list.

Sub-options exist for each type of chart.

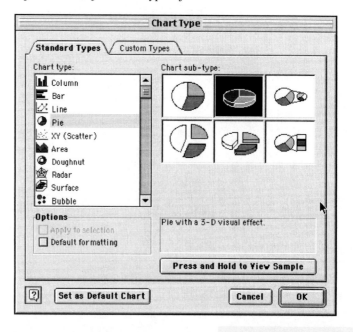

172

◆ Double-click the format you prefer in the **Chart sub-type** frame.

Adding a title

◆ **Chart**
Chart Options
Titles tab

◆ Click the text box corresponding to the sort of title you want to insert.

◆ Enter your title.

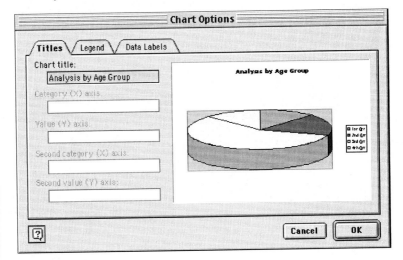

◆ Click **OK**.

Modifying labels

◆ **Chart**
Chart Options
Data Labels tab

◆ Indicate how the **Data Labels** should be displayed.

◆ Click **OK**.

Managing the legend

◆ **Chart**
Chart Options
Legend tab

◆ Choose whether or not to display the legend by activating or deactivating the **Show legend** option.

◆ Use the options under **Placement** to position the legend.

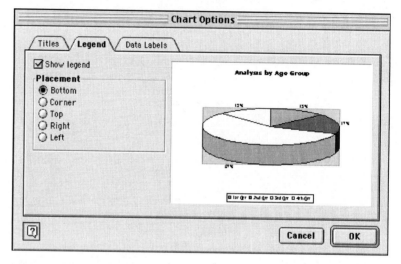

◆ Click **OK**.

Changing the border/colour/shading of the bars/sectors

◆ Select the item to be modified.

◆ Double-click the item.

◆ Make sure that the dialog box is open at the **Patterns** page.

◆ Choose a **Border**.

◆ Under **Area**, choose the color and/or the pattern.

◆ Click **OK**.

Exploding a slice from a pie chart

◆ Click the slice concerned twice (not a double-click but slowly) to select it.

◆ Drag the slice out from the chart (by the middle of the slice).

Formatting characters

◆ Select the characters concerned.

◆ **Format
   Font...**

◆ Activate the attributes you require.

◆ Click **OK**.

Leaving Microsoft Graph

♦ Click in the document outside the chart.

❏ *To edit the chart, double-click it.*

Once you have left Microsoft Graph you may find that your chart object appears as a field code. To make this object appear as a chart, click **Tools - Preferences** and deactivate the **Field Codes** option on the **View** tab.

. . . . *Personal notes* . . . .

Creating a form

A form is a document containing permanent text and spaces for filling in variable data.

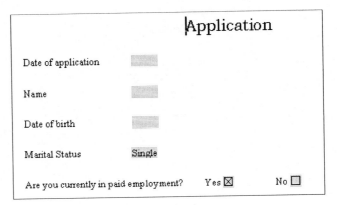

♦ Go into creation of a <u>template</u> (**File - New**, **General** tab, **Template** option).

♦ Enter the permanent text.

♦ Insert a form field wherever you want to collect information (see below).

♦ Protect the completed form.

Inserting form fields

*A **form field** can be presented as a check box, an edit box (text field) or a combo box (an edit box combined with a pop-up menu).*

♦ Display the **Forms** toolbar.

♦ Place the insertion point where the field should appear.

♦ Click the **abl** button to insert an edit box, the ☑ button for a check box or the button for a combo box.

The form is inserted into the document. For example, a grey rectangle is inserted for a text field.

♦ Click 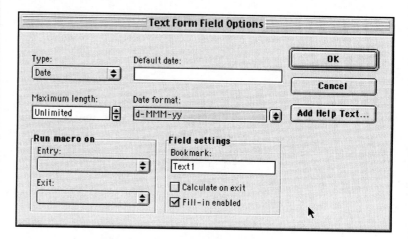 to set the options for the field.

A text field

♦ Click the **ab** button, then 📇.

♦ Specify the **Type** of text field.

♦ If you want to display a short help message on the status bar, click the **Add Help Text** button, and type the text in the **Type your own** box.

♦ Click **OK**.

❏ *The field inserted is called {FORMTEXT}.*

A combination edit box - pop-up menu

♦ Place the insertion point where you want the list to appear.

♦ Click 🖼 then 📇.

♦ For each item you want in the list:

- enter its name in the **Drop-down item** box,

- click the **Add** button.

♦ If you wish to remove an item, select it in the **Items in drop-down list** box then click the **Remove** button.

♦ If you need to, reorganise the list displayed in **Items in drop-down list** using the two **Move** buttons.

♦ Click **Add Help Text** if you wish to display a message.

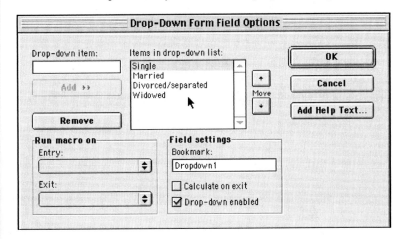

♦ Click **OK**.

The first item in the list is always proposed by default.

❑ *The field inserted is called {FORMDROPDOWN}.*

A check box

♦ Position the insertion point where the check box is to appear.

♦ Click to insert the field, then click .

♦ Specify how you want the check box to look.

♦ If you wish, click **Add Help Text** to enter a help message.

♦ Click **OK**.

❑ The field inserted is called {FORMCHECKBOX}.

❑ These three form fields can be used only if the document is protected as a form (see below).

Protecting the form

♦ Make sure that the document is completely finished.

♦ **Tools**
  Protect Document...

♦ Activate the **Forms** option (under **Protect document for**).

♦ If you wish, enter a **Password** with a maximum of 15 characters.

Protect Document

Protect document for
○ Tracked changes
○ Comments
● Forms: Sections...

Password (optional):
●●●

Cancel   OK

On the screen, the characters of the password are always repla-ced by dots. Be careful about the case of the letters you use.

♦ Click **OK**.

To ensure against mistakes, you must repeat your password in the dialog box which appears.

♦ Enter the password and click **OK**.

❑ *The* *tool allows you to protect/unprotect a form without set-ting a password.*

---

*To remove the protection, use **Tools - Unprotect Document** and enter the password.*
Be careful about the case of the characters.

Using a form

♦ Create a document based on a form template.

The first form field is selected, and its help text is displayed on the status bar.

Because the document is protected as a form, access is authori-sed only to form fields.

♦ Move from field to field using ⊟→⊟ and (⇧ Shift) ⊟→⊟, and fill in the data.

❑ *You can copy the content of one text field, then paste it into another.*

Using a document/ template with form fields

This type of document is one which is printed several times, but with only a few variations each time. Two types of fields may be defined: use an ASK field if you want to use a piece of data several times in a document, or a FILLIN field to print the data just once.

Creating the document/template

♦ Enter the document's permanent text.

♦ Insert ASK fields and/or FILLIN fields (use an ASK field if you are going to use the data supplied by the user more than once).

Inserting an ASK field

♦ Position the insertion point at the beginning of the document.

♦ Press ⌘ F9 .

♦ Enter the syntax for the field:
ASK [space] field-name [space] "Message".

"Message" is the prompt text which appears in the dialog box to facilitate filling in the information.

♦ At each point in the text where data input is needed, press ⌘ F9 and insert the field name.

Inserting a FILLIN field

♦ At each point in the text where data input is needed, press ⌘ F9 .

♦ Enter the syntax for the field:
FILLIN [space] "Message".

{ { ask name "enter title and name" } }

{ name }
{ fillin "address" }

Dear { name }|

I am delighted to tell you that you have been selected to take part in our Grand Prize Draw !
Just look at the fabulous prizes we are offering ! The draw will take place on the { fillin "date" } : still
another few weeks to contain your excitement !

Your lucky number is { fillin "Number" }.

It could well be one of the big winners !

We wish you the very best of luck !

Jack Harrington
Customer Satisfaction Manager

Filling in a document/template with form fields

♦ Create a new document based on the template concerned, or open the document concerned.

♦ Select the whole document.

♦ Press ⌨F9 to fill in the (FILLIN) fields.

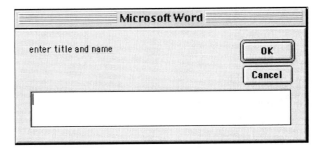

♦ In response to the prompt message, type in the data, pressing ⏎ to move down to a new line. Click **OK** after each response.

♦ Fill in all the fields in the same way.

❑ You can also fill in the form fields as the document is printing. Wherever Word meets an **ASK** field or a **FILLIN** field, it displays a dialog box where you enter data in response to a prompt message (providing that the **Update fields** option is active on the **Print** page of the **Tools - Preferences** dialog box).

. . . . Personal notes . . . .

**Planning
a mail merge**

*The **mail merge** allows you to send out a large number of copies of a document to a list of addresses contained in a data file.*

◆ Two files are used in this technique:

— a **data source** file containing the variable information.

— a **main document** containing the permanent text.

◆ A data source file is made up of **fields** and **records**.
For example:

1st name	Surname	Address	Town	Postcode
Maurice	DALTON	3 Apostle St	Reading	RG2 4JR
Anne	VINCENT	9 Queens Rd	Manchester	M20 6ST

Each line of information constitutes a record. Each column is a field.

◆ The records are numbered. The numbers correspond to the order in which they were entered, or to a sort order applied later.

◆ Plan the data source file by noting all the information you need. For the preceding example, five fields will be needed: the first name, the surname, the address, the town and the postcode.

Creating the main source document

◆ If you wish, begin by entering the permanent text, and its formatting, as a document.

◆ **Tools
Mail Merge**

For the moment, you can work only in the first area: creating the *Main document*.

♦ Click the **Create** button, then choose **Form Letters**.

♦ If you have already entered the permanent text, click **Active Window**, otherwise choose **New Main Document**.

*After this, the **Get Data** button becomes accessible.*

♦ If you want to work on your main document, click **Close**, otherwise keep the dialog box open.

Using a data source file

♦ Open the main document, and go to the **Tools - Mail Merge** dialog box.

♦ Click the **Get Data** button.

♦ Indicate whether you wish to **Create Data Source** or **Open Data Source**.

*If you click **Open Data Source**, Word produces a list of existing data files. Double-click the one you want to use.*

Creating a data source file

♦ Activate the main document; go into the **Tools - Mail Merge** dialog box; click **Get Data** then **Create Data Source**.

♦ In the **Field names in header row** list, Word proposes a list of commonly-used names. Click each field you do not need, then click the **Remove Field Name** button.

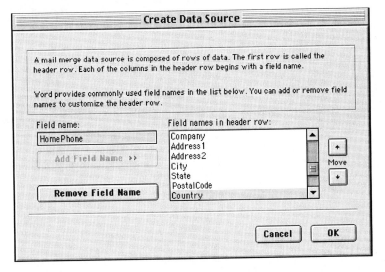

♦ If you need to create additional fields, delete the name in the **Field name** box if necessary, type in the name of your own field, then click **Add Field Name**.

Any new fields you create are added at the end of the list.
It is preferable for fields to appear in the order they will have in the document.

♦ If you want to move a field, select it in the **Field names in header row** list then use the **Move** arrows.

♦ When you have finished designing your data source file, click **OK**.

♦ Enter the name of the file.

Word detects that this file is empty of data, and proposes that you edit the data.

♦ Click the **Edit Data Source** button.

Word displays a blank data form.

♦ For each record:

– Type in the data using 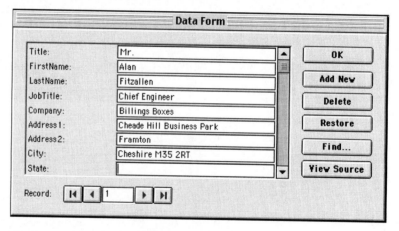 to move to the next text box and ⇧ Shift ↹ to return to the previous one,

– After the last line press ↵ if you want to create another new record.

♦ End by clicking the **OK** button.

You return to the main document.

❑ *In the main document, the **Mail Merge** toolbar is displayed. It proposes various Mail Merge functions.*

Inserting a field

♦ Place the insertion point where the contents of the field are to be printed.

♦ Click the **Insert Merge Field** button on the Merge bar.

All the fields of the data file are listed.

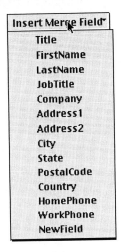

♦ Click the field you need to insert.

❏ *You can click the* *button to check the merge.*

Carrying out the mail merge

♦ Open the main document:

 sends the merge to the printer.

 sends the merge to a new document, which Word names "form Letter n".

**Limiting
the merge
to predefined
records**

♦ From the main document go into:

Tools
Mail Merge
Merge button

♦ In the **Merge to** box, specify whether or not the merge is to go straight to the printer.

♦ In the **Records to be merged** frame, give the number of the first record concerned, then that of the last.

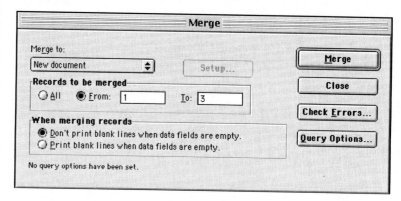

♦ Click the **Merge** button.

**Setting out
conditions
for a mail merge**

♦ From the main document:

Tools
Mail Merge
Merge button

♦ Click the **Query Options** button.

♦ If necessary, activate the **Filter Records** tab.

♦ For each condition set:

– select the name of the field in the **Field** list,

– if appropriate, specify the operator for the comparison in the **Comparison** list,

– if appropriate, click the **Compare to** box and type in the value,

– if there are no other conditions, click **OK**,

– if there is another condition, choose the combination operator from the list where **And** is displayed by default.

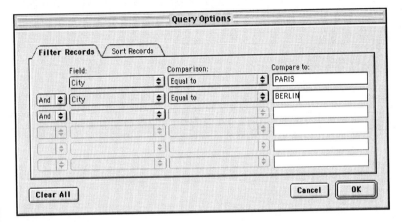

♦ Click the **OK** button when you have finished.

♦ Carry out the mail merge, or put it on hold with the **Close** button.

❑ *The conditions set are saved in the main document.*

To cancel the conditions set, click the **Clear All** button in the **Query Options** dialog box.

**Managing
records**

Displaying the data form

♦ Click 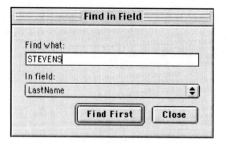.

The data form is displayed along with the first record.

Adding a record

♦ Display the form.

*Notice that number 1 is displayed in the **Record** box.*

♦ Click the **Add New** button.

*A blank data form appears and the number of the active **Record**
changes.*

♦ Enter the new record in the same way as the others.

Finding a record

♦ Display the data form.

♦ Display the first record.

♦ Click the **Find** button.

♦ In the **Find what** box, enter the value you are looking for.

♦ Use the **In field** pop-up menu to choose the name of the field
containing that value.

♦ Start the search by **Find First**, then **Find Next** as many times as it takes to find the right record.

Deleting a record

♦ Display the form.

♦ Display the record you wish to delete.

♦ Click **Delete**.

❏*Be very careful when deleting a record, as it is destroyed immediately: you are not prompted for confirmation.*

Modifying a record

♦ Display the form.

♦ Display the record concerned.

♦ Carry out the changes.

♦ If there is an error in the new version, click **Restore** to return to the original.

♦ When you have finished editing the data file, click **OK**.

To change the structure of the data file (the order of the fields...), open the data file in the same way as any document (the records have been entered in the form of a table). Modify the file then save it.

Sorting a data file

♦ Open the main document.

♦ **Tools**
Mail Merge
Merge button

♦ Click **Query Options**.

♦ If necessary, activate the **Sort Records** tab.

A data file can be sorted by up to three fields.

♦ For each of these, open the **Sort by** pop-up menu, click the name of the field and specify whether the records should be sorted in **Ascending** or **Descending** order.

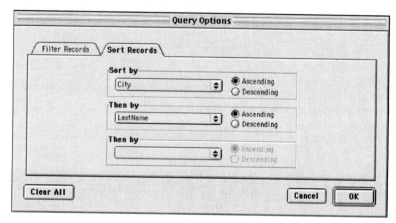

♦ Click **OK**.

Printing mailing labels

♦ Open a new document.

♦ **Tools**
   Mail Merge

♦ Click the **Create** button under **Main document**.

♦ Choose **Mailing Labels**.

♦ Click **Active Window**.

♦ Click the **Get Data** button under **Data Source**. Choose either to **Create Data Source** or to **Open Data Source**.

Word analyses the first record then prompts you to return to the main document.

♦ Click **Set Up Main Document.**

♦ Use the **Label Options** window and, if necessary, the **Label products** pop-up menu to define the details of your labels.

♦ Click **OK.**

♦ Choose each element you need on the label from the **Insert Merge Field** pop-up menu, then do the formatting in the **Sample label** box.

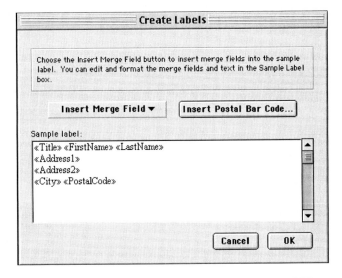

♦ Once the label is finished to your satisfaction, click **OK.**

♦ Click the **Close** button.

A page of labels appears:

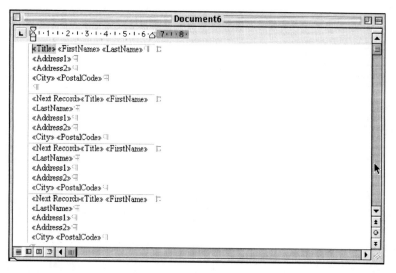

❏ *The labels are printed in the same way as any mail merge: a label is just a special sort of main document.*

Controlling blank lines in a merge

♦ **Tools**
Mail Merge
click **Merge**

♦ Use the **When merging records** options to tell Word what to do with blank lines.
Choose between **Don't print blank lines when data fields are empty** and **Print blank lines when data fields are empty**.

♦ Start the merge by clicking **Merge**, or click **Close** to put it on hold.

Setting conditions for inserting a text

♦ Place the insertion point where the text is to appear.

♦ Click the **Insert Word Field** button then the **If ... Then ... Else** option.

♦ Enter your condition using the **Field name**, **Comparison** and **Compare to** lists.

♦ In the **Insert this text** box, enter the text which will be printed if the condition is satisfied.

♦ Then use the **Otherwise insert this text** box to enter a text which will be printed if the condition is not satisfied.

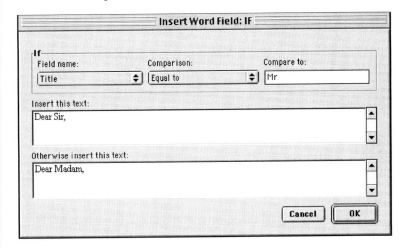

♦ Finish by clicking the **OK** button.

Example: {IF MERGEFIELD TITLE}= "Mr" "Dear Sir" "Dear Madam"}

If the field code display is no longer active, display the codes by pressing [⇥][F9] *to read what you have just created.*

Setting conditions for the insertion of a document

♦ Place the insertion point where you wish the document to appear.

♦ Insert an **IF** field, then for each action insert an INCLUDETEXT field.
The syntax is: **INCLUDETEXT File_name**
Example: {IF{MERGEFIELD THANKS}= "-1"
"{INCLUDETEXT GIFT}" "{INCLUDETEXT GIFT5}"}

. . . . *Personal notes* . . . .

Creating a macro

♦ Use the template concerned (**Normal** is chosen by default).

♦ **Tools**
Macro
Record New Macro...

♦ Give the macro a name in the **Macro name** box.

♦ Use the **Store macro in** list to choose the folder where you want to save the macro.

♦ If you wish, enter a **Description**.

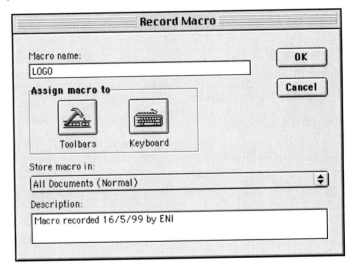

♦ Specify whether you want to run the macro by clicking a tool button (**Toolbars**) or by pressing a shortcut key (**Keyboard**).

♦ If you have chosen **Toolbars**, display if necessary the toolbar you would like to use and drag the macro from the **Commands** list in the **Customize** dialog box onto the bar, then click **Close**.

The Macro toolbar appears in a window, and the letters REC appear in black on the status bar.

♦ Go through all the actions to be recorded in the macro.

♦ When you have finished, click .

The letters REC on the status bar become dim.

Running a macro

♦ Use the tool button or the keys that you have assigned to your macro.

> *If you prefer to run a macro by its name, go into **Macros** or press ⌘ F8 . Click **Tools - Macros**, Word then lists all the existing macros. Click the name of the macro you need, and then **Run**.*

Editing a macro

♦ **Tools**
  Macro
  Macros...

♦ ⌘ F8

♦ In **Macro name**, click the macro you need to modify.

♦ Click the **Edit** button.

Macros are written in Visual Basic. For example :

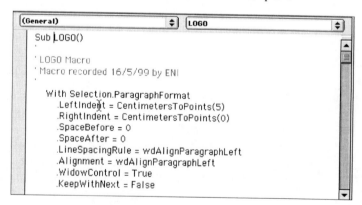

```
(General)                        ♦  LOGO                           ♦

Sub LOGO()

' LOGO Macro
' Macro recorded 16/5/99 by ENI

    With Selection.ParagraphFormat
        .LeftIndent = CentimetersToPoints(5)
        .RightIndent = CentimetersToPoints(0)
        .SpaceBefore = 0
        .SpaceAfter = 0
        .LineSpacingRule = wdAlignParagraphLeft
        .Alignment = wdAlignParagraphLeft
        .WidowControl = True
        .KeepWithNext = False
```

♦ Carry out the modifications.

♦ **File**
  Close and Return to Microsoft Word

Deleting a macro

♦ **Tools**
  Macro
  Macros...

♦

♦ Click the name of the macro you wish to delete in **Macro name**.

♦ Click the **Delete** button and confirm by **Yes**.

♦ Click **Close**.

. . . . *Personal notes* . . . .

Formatting

Characters

⌘ ⇧Shift F	Selecting a font
⌘ ⇧Shift > / ⌘ ⇧Shift <	Next size up/down
⇧Shift F3	Change the case of letters
⌘ B	Bold formatting
⌘ ⇧Shift H	Activate/deactivate hidden text
⌘ I	Italic formatting
⌘ ⇧Shift K	Format as small capitals
⌘ U	Underline
⌘ ⇧Shift W	Underline individual words
⌘ ⇧Shift D	Double underline
⌘ ⇧Shift +	Superscript
⌘ =	Subscript
Ctrl space	Normal character
⌘ ⇧Shift Q	Symbol font

Paragraphs

⌘ 1 / ⌘ 2	Single/Double line spacing
⌘ 5	1.5 line spaces between lines
⌘ 0 (zero)	Add/delete a blank line before the paragraph
⌘ E	Centre a paragraph
⌘ L	Left Align
⌘ R	Right Align
⌘ J	Justify a paragraph
⌘ M / ⌘ ⇧Shift M	Increase/decrease left indent
⌘ T / ⌘ ⇧Shift T	Increase/decrease hanging indent of first line
⌘ ⇥ Q	Standard Paragraph

Various

⌘ ⇧Shift N	Return to Normal style
⌘ ⇧Shift C	Copy formatting
⌘ ⇧Shift V	Paste formatting
⇥ ⌘ K	Run autoformat
⇥ ⌘ 1	Apply style Heading1
⇥ ⌘ 2	Apply style Heading2
⇥ ⌘ 3	Apply style Heading3

Moving/selecting/entering text

⇧ ⌘ ←   Delete the word to the left of the insertion point
⇧ ⌘ Del   Delete the word to the right of the insertion point

Moving

↓ / ↑   Following/preceding line
→ / ←   Following/preceding character
↘ / ↖   End/beginning of a line
Pg Up / Pg Dn   Previous/following screen
⇧ ⌘ ↖ / ⇧ ⌘ ↘   Beginning/end of the document
⇧ ⌘ ⇥ Pg Up / ⇧ ⌘ ⇥ Pg Dn   Top/bottom of the window

⇧ ⌘ ↑ / ⇧ ⌘ ↓   Previous/following paragraph

Selecting

F 8   Select text/columns
⇧ Shift F 8   Return to previous selection
⇧ ⌘ A   Select whole document

Inserting special characters/contents

⇧ Shift ↵   Line break
⇥ ⌐   Page break
⇧ ⌘ ⇧ Shift ↵   Column break
⇧ ⌘ -   Conditional hyphen
⇥ ⇧ ⌘ V   Insert AutoText
Ctrl ⇧ Shift T   Insert time field
Ctrl ⇧ Shift D   Insert date field
Ctrl ⇧ Shift P   Insert page field
⇥ C   Copyright symbol
⇥ R   Registered Trademark symbol
⇥ ⇧ Shift T   Trademark symbol

Specific shortcut keys

Fields

F9
Ō ⌘ F9
⇧ Shift F9 / ⇥ F9
F11
⇧ Shift F11

Update selected field
Insert a field
Display/hide a selected field code/all field codes
Go to next field
Go to previous field

Tables

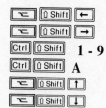

→| / ⇧ Shift →|
⇥ Ō ⌘ T
⇥ ↘ / ⇥ ↖
⇥ Pg Dn / ⇥ Pg Up

Select next/previous cell
Select whole table
Go to the last/first cell of the line
Go to the last/first cell of the column

Outlines

⇥ ⇧ Shift ←
⇥ ⇧ Shift →
Ctrl ⇧ Shift **1 - 9**
Ctrl ⇧ Shift **A**
⇥ ⇧ Shift ↑
⇥ ⇧ Shift ↓
Ō ⌘ ⇧ Shift F6

Level +1
Level -1
Display by heading level
Display whole document (heading, Sub-heading, texts)
Move a heading towards the one before
Move a heading towards the one after
Activate the last window

Window

Ō ⌘ F6
Ō ⌘ ⇧ Shift F6

Go to the next window
Go to the previous window

Mail Merges

Ctrl ⇧ Shift **K**
Ctrl ⇧ Shift **N**
Ctrl ⇧ Shift **M**
Ctrl ⇧ Shift **E**
Ctrl ⇧ Shift **F**

Preview a mail merge
Merge to a new document
Print a merged document
Modify the data file
Insert a merge field

Menu shortcut keys

File

New...

Open...

Close

Save

Print...

Exit

Print preview

Save as

Edit

Undo

Repeat

Cut

Copy

Paste

Select All

Go To ...

Find

Replace

View

Normal

Outline

Page Layout

Insert

Footnote

Endnote

Mark index entry

Hyperlink

Format

Font...

AutoFormat...

`⇧ Shift` `F7`	**Tools**
`F7`	Thesaurus...
`Alt` `F8`	Spelling check
`Alt` `F11`	Macros
	Visual Basic Editor

Tools

Thesaurus...
Spelling check
Macros
Visual Basic Editor

`⌐` click
`⌂` `⌘` `⌐` T

Table

Select column
Select table

Various shortcut keys

`⇧ Shift` `F10`
`⇧ Shift` `F5`
`⇧ Shift` `F4`
`⇧ Shift` `F2` / `F2`
`F6` / `⇧ Shift` `F6`
`⌂` `⌘` !

Displays a shortcut menu
Return to last three positions
Reruns a search
Copy/move text without using clipboard
Move to next/previous pane
Display/hide non-printing characters

See also TABS, PAGE SETUP

G

GRAMMAR   Checking   123

H

HEADER   *See PAGE SETUP*

HYPERLINK   Inserting   41

HYPHENATION   Hyphenating Words   131

I

INDEX   *See TABLES*

S

T

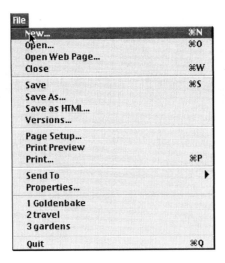

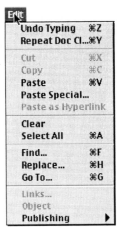

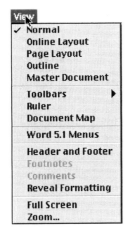

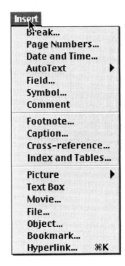

Format

Font...	⌘D
Paragraph...	⌘⌥M
Document...	

Bullets and Numbering...
Borders and Shading...

Columns...
Tabs...
Drop Cap...
Text Direction...
Change Case...

AutoFormat...
Style Gallery...
Style...
Background

Object...

Tools

Spelling and Grammar.	⌘⌥L
Language	▶

Word Count...
AutoSummarize...
AutoCorrect...

Track Changes ▶
Merge Documents...
Protect Document...

Mail Merge...
Envelopes and Labels...
Letter Wizard...

Macro ▶
Templates and Add-Ins...
Customize...
Preferences...

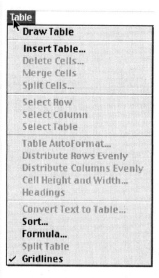

Table

Draw Table

Insert Table...
Delete Cells...
Merge Cells
Split Cells...

Select Row
Select Column
Select Table

Table AutoFormat...
Distribute Rows Evenly
Distribute Columns Evenly
Cell Height and Width...
Headings

Convert Text to Table...
Sort...
Formula...
Split Table
✓ Gridlines

Window

New Window
Arrange All
Split
Show Clipboard
✓ 1 Document1

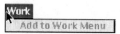

Help

About Balloon Help...

Show Balloons

Microsoft Word Help

Contents and Index

Help on the Web
Online Registration

Work

Add to Work Menu